The Food and Art
of Azerbaijan

This book is dedicated to three most important women in my life and my family – my grandmother Almaz, my aunt Rahshanda and my mother Ulduz. This book is based on their favourite recipes.

The Food and Art of Azerbaijan

Khabiba Kashkay

UNICORN PRESS LTD

Azerbaijan

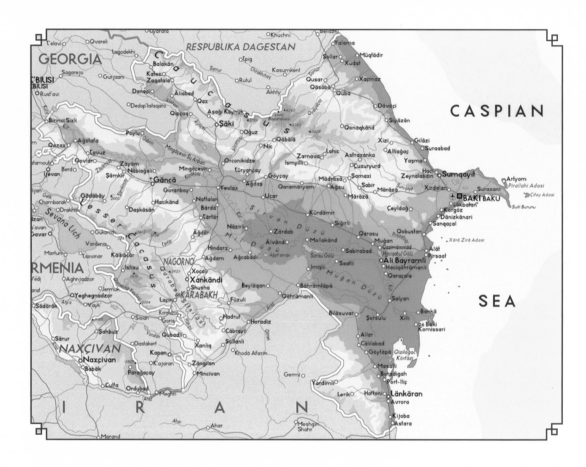

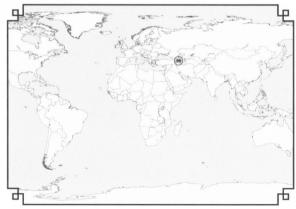

Contents

Summer

Autumn

Winter

Marinades and Sauces   462

Additional Recipes   498

Introduction

The idea of writing about the delicious food of Azerbaijan for the Russian reader was not accidental. Whenever I visit Moscow's book shops I admire the lively and genuine interest of the Russians in the history and culture of other nations. There you see many books about history, art, and music but also now increasingly books about cuisine. The French, Italian, Indian, Thai, Chinese, Korean, Japanese and Moroccan and many others are all well represented. Nevertheless, I also noticed that little is known about the cooking traditions of Azerbaijan, which is now an independent country, located at the crossroads of Europe and Asia.

Azerbaijan is a very beautiful country situated on the ridges and valleys of the Greater and Lesser Caucasus and the Caspian Sea, stretching from the borders of Russia to Iran. There is much more to Azerbaijan than its famous oil reserves! The Great Silk Road runs through Azerbaijan. It is known as the "The Land of the Fire" due to the unquenchable flames coming from the bowels of the earth. In the sixteenth century Indian fire worshippers paved the way there, followers of the Zoroastrians who built the Temple of Fire, Ateshgiah, today a famous tourist attraction. It has always had a fascinating history, being the battleground between the empires of Russia and Persia. More recently it experienced the Soviet era, and today it is an independent state successfully integrated into the modern world.

Azerbaijan is also a country with a unique climate. It is like a miniature model of the planet: the eternal snows of the Greater Caucasus are combined with the golden beaches of the Caspian Sea. The land is rich in culture, literature, and great music. Azerbaijan is also a country of magnificent paintings and amazingly delicious food.

This book is dedicated to Azerbaijani cuisine. The recipes described here are home-cooked meals that have been prepared in my family for generations and will I hope be passed on to future generations. The features of the country described above have created a diverse and broad palette of taste, which creates the uniqueness of Azerbaijani cuisine. Therefore, there are many ingredients; from a variety of spices and herbs to the magnificent fruits and vegetables, which are an integral part of Azerbaijani dishes. Pomegranate, quince, sharon fruit, peach and apricot were attributed magical properties from ancient times, contributing to the preservation of health and youth. No accident that in Medieval Azerbaijani poetry such as that by Nizami, the cheeks of a beautiful girl were compared with a velvet peach. Quince was believed to improve longevity, and its water infused seeds healed coughs and bronchitis. Pomegranate gave strength, because it is a blood-forming fruit, and it has many other healing properties. Saffron, also known as the elixir of youth, is an indispensable ingredient of Azerbaijani cuisine. It is not a coincidence that Azerbaijan is a country where there are many centenarians – food plays an important role in long life.

I named the book Azerbaijani Food and Art, its Practice during the Four Seasons.

The rich traditions of Azerbaijani painting began in the Paleolithic Age. In Gobustan, near Baku, more than four thousand paintings survive, created by primitive painters, in what has been called an art gallery. Medieval Azerbaijani miniatures are well known and appreciated all over the world. A powerful school of modernist painting began in the 20th Century and still continues today.

The art of cooking has always gone hand in hand with other art forms, especially painting. People always decorated their houses and homes, hanging pictures on the walls, laying tables artistically and preparing food which was not only delicious, but also beautiful. A variety of dishes, in their appearance and their placing on the table, can remind us of a beautiful painting.

In creating a particular dish we are layering strokes akin to an artist using a palette. Therefore, while choosing dishes from this book I think you will be interested to see a number of masterpieces and very good paintings by Azerbaijani artists. The paintings are all from our family collection, mainly from the 20th Century. The 20th Century for Azerbaijani art has been called a golden age. Works of Satar Bahlulzade, Tahir Salahov, Togrul Narimanbekov, Nadir Abdurachmanov and a number of others that you will see in this book are found in many museums and private collections.

I divided the book into four seasons. Each chapter consists of dishes specific to the time of year, but that does not mean you cannot prepare dishes from other parts of the book. I chose the paintings to complement the seasons and to demonstrate the beauty of Azerbaijan. Thanks to the magnificent pictorial art you can appreciate this wonderful country, its people, its nature, the Caspian Sea, the magnificent Caucasus, and, of course, the FOOD. With these pictures you can stroll through the seasons of the year with the preparation of delicious, healthy and beautiful food, as well as taking a small tour of the masterpieces of Azerbaijani art.

And the conclusion…

Azerbaijani cuisine is rich in regional traditions (of Baku, Ganzja, Karabakh, Kuba, Nakhchivan, Lankaran, Shamakha etc.) I have tried to create the most typical dishes of the Azerbaijani traditions of cooking, reproducing a number of old recipes that have survived in my family. In this book, 80 per cent of the recipes are for everyday cooking, while the rest are for festive meals. I have described a set of quick, easy to make recipes for everyday, along with time-consuming meals for special occasions.

Azerbaijani food has many sweet and sour flavours, especially from the abundant fruit and spicy greens. Pomegranates have a special place in the cuisine, and there are more than one thousand varieties in Azerbaijan. A plate of greens and fresh vegetables on the table adds great flavour and guarantees good digestion.

Despite the fact that desserts occupy an important place in Azerbaijani cuisine, no lunch

is considered complete without a good dish of goat, cow or sheep milk Bryndza (a variety of Caucasian cheese).

The cuisine is attractive to both those who wish to eat healthy food as well as to connoisseurs of fine delicate cooking. There are many dishes to satisfy both meat eaters and vegetarians. The climate and flora of Azerbaijan contribute to the creation of a rich mosaic of tastes, i.e. cereals, herbs, fruit and vegetables, to be made into many healthy and delicious dishes for vegetarians.

Dear reader, I would love to have this book become a starting point for your own imagination, enabling you to create new dishes based on the taste palette of Azerbaijani cuisine. The ability to cook and improvise is a kind of magic!

A Practical Guide to all Seasons

Salads

Salads in Azerbaijani cuisine are very peculiar. They are prepared with vinegar, pomegranate juice, cherries and cherry juice, or extract of cherry-plum etc. They are characterised by the use of large amounts of greens. Hot and cold appetisers with eggs, fried onions, and roasted vegetables are of special interest. Casseroles made of greens, aubergines, potatoes and eggs are really unique.

Soups

Traditionally, a large number of Azerbaijani first courses are very thick. It is not even necessary to serve second courses after them. Some of them are cooked in saucepans and some in clay ramekins in a stove or oven. Dishes made of organic homemade yoghurt (katyk) go especially well in summer heat.

Flour dishes/soups are cooked mainly with water or broth in the winter. They are perfect when you get colds (especially soups with homemade noodles (arishta) that miraculously fight off coughs). There is a recipe provided below for preparing dough for different flour dishes, however to save time you can use ready-made noodles, like vermicelli. Some dishes, like small ravioli (diushbara), require just prepared and rolled out dough.

Peas are used in a number of dishes, therefore the recipes for cooking peas are provided separately. The word 'shorba', which appears in several names of main courses, is a special type of thick soup, where peas, all types of dry lobio and frain are used. The word 'shorba'

mean 'pohliobka' in Russian language and it is known as 'pottage to the Europeans. That is why in the "Winter" section a few soup recipes are presented as a main dish with meat.

Meat

Each of 39 regions of Azerbaijan has its own zest in cooking meat dishes. The privilege is given to lamb meat, mutton, beef, calf, and game. The impeccable flavour of these dishes is achieved thanks to special recipes, abundance of greens and vegetables, herbs and spices.

Poultry

The Azerbaijani cuisine is has its own national colour, which is expressed in the specifics of the cuisine techniques for preparation of dishes and traditions of the Azerbaijani tables.

Thus, poultry dishes in the national cuisine are generally prepared with vegetables, eggs, herbs, fruit sauces and nuts in various selections.

Some of them are given in this book.

Kebabs

Kebab is one of the most favourite dishes in Azerbaijan prepared without the addition of water. The Russian name – shashlik – comes from the word shishlik, i.e. food strung on a skewer. Shashlik is generally prepared from young lamb or yeanling (meat of a male is tastier) on a brazier with hot coals. If the grease dripping from the skewer creates a flame, it is sprinkled with salty water. If the coals cool down, they should be fanned. Shashliks receive their names based on the method of preparation of meat, type of meat and offal, as well as vegetables and fish. The most tender shashlik is prepared with meat made with the bastyrma method 18-20 hours or a whole day prior to cooking. Bastyrma is prepared as follows: cut the meat into slices. Take 1.5 kg of onions for 4 kg of meat, chop them, add salt, mix with the meat and lay in an enamelled pot for a day. Leave the pot outside the refrigerator but in a cool place. When preparing the shashlik remove the onion from the meat and string it on skewers. Bastyrma can even be prepared from veal, beef, heart and kidneys.

Meat of wild animals (deer, mountain-goat), liver, ram testis are better when strung on the skewers right away, without preparation of basturma.

Brazier (barbecue) is prepared as follows. Make a fire and wait until the coal or wood in the barbecue reach smouldering coal state. The heat should be intense.

Offal dishes

The Azerbaijani national cuisine uses almost all types of offal: liver, kidney, heart, intestine, stomach, testis, craw. The variety of cooking methods that follow allow you to experience the wide range of different tastes. The use of fat tail of lamb gives an exceptional taste to offal dishes.

Fish

Dishes made with sea, river and lake fish are traditional for the Azerbaijani cuisine. One of the most delicious fish – Kutum (a Caspian kind of carp) – lives in the Caspian Sea like Sturgeon.

Asp, zander and shamaya are caught in the Kura river, trout can be caught in mountain rivers.

Fish dishes are prepared in oven, furnace, open fire with seasonings, dried fruits, nuts.

Pilaffs

One of the most delicious, colourful and festive dishes of the Azerbaijani cuisine is the pilaff (ash) with over 100 varieties. The serving of pilaff itself is a special ritual, since the Azerbaijani pilaff is a dish of many components. There are more complex types of pilaff (for holidays and other celebrations) as well as simpler and basic ones.

There are two methods for preparing the rice – filtering, gluten free (siuzmya ash) and draught (checkmya ash). For most types of pilaff the long grain rice is used. The choice of method determines the variety of pilaff, name, taste, as well as the look of the pilaff.

Mandatory conditions for all types of pilaff:
1. The pot should be made of copper or aluminium. In any other pot the pilaff will be bunt. It is best to use a pot with a conic form.
2. Long rice should be used – Basmati, Khan, Pakistani, Lenkoran, Vietnamese with Jasmine.
3. The rice should be soaked in very salty water for 4-5 hours, preferably overnight. The water should cover the rice by about 3-4 fingers deep.
4. Before cooking the rice, it should be rinsed thoroughly.
5. The filtered rice (siuzmya ash) should be cooked in a large pan, with the calculation of 1 cup of rice to 3 cups of water. You need to cook the rice for 6 minutes until it is half done. The rice should be quite loose and not stick or form lumps.

6. Then place the half cooked rice into a colander to get rid of water. The rice should go back into the pan and laid on the crust ("Kazmag", please see below). Please add saffron which you prepare in advance and zira or thyme spice on the top of the rice. Then pour 50g of melted butter over the saffron and put the rice on a low heat for an hour to cook using an absorbtion method under the lid.

7. The lid of the pan should be wrapped in a cotton towel so the condensation does not fall back into the rice after it has risen to the lid, but gets soaked into the towel.

8. If there are no appetisers before the pilaff, allow 1 cup of rice per person, if there are appetisers then ½ cup should be sufficient.

9. Azerbaijani pilaff is eaten with a spoon and always has a special side dish either meat, chicken, fish, vegetables or dried fruits.

Crust under Pilaffs – Kazmag

Kazmag (crust) is always prepared for the filtered (siuzmya) pilaff. It protects the rice from getting burned. When pilaff is served onto a dish, the kazmag is taken from the bottom of the pan and placed on a separate plate or put around the pilaff on the dish. Several types of kazmag can be made.

You may purchase a ready-made lavash at the supermarket, pour 1-1½ tablespoons of melted butter into the pan, lay the lavash (thicker one) in one layer. Then all the components of pilaff are laid down as said in the recipes.

Second method of preparing Kazmag is as follows: peel 3-4 average potatoes, cut them into 0.5 cm thick disks. Pour some oil into the

pan, heat it, sprinkle some salt and lay one layer of the potato disks onto the bottom of the pan. Move them around to prevent sticking and then proceed as said in the pilaff recipes. You can use the crust with every pilaff recipe in this book, in order to avoid burning the rice.

Dough and Porridge dishes

These dishes are prepared with flavourless stiff dough, which is rolled very thin, a little thicker than a sheet of paper. To roll such dough, normally the long double-edged rolling pin.

Porridges incorporate almost all kinds of grain, but more often the wheat, rice are used, as well as flour, many various beans. Porridges are prepared with large amounts of various seasonings – saffron, rose extract, turmeric, cinnamon, cumin, etc.

The Azerbaijani cuisine has various flour based dishes: diushbara, fiasiali, kutab, giurza, chudu, etc.

Dough for hot flour dishes – dushbara, arishta, gurza, sulu hangal, and hangal.

2 cups of flour
1 egg
Water – as much as necessary
Salt, to taste
Heap the flour, make a well in the middle, crack in an egg inside the well, add water, and knead the dough.

The dough should be stiff. Divide the dough into small lumps, roll it out very thin (1 mm), and leave it for a while. Cut the thin noodles (arishta) as follows: fold a sheet of dough a few times and cut it into very thin slices – 1-2 mm in width. Then sprinkle a little flour on it and let it dry. It can be used for several months.

The same dough is used for sulu hangyal, thin dough sheet is cut into small squares 5 mm in width, then dried and used as needed. The same for hangyal (that is the second course), but the dough sheets are cut into diamonds 3-4 cm in width (a little elongated).

For the small meat ravioli (diushbara), cut the just prepared sheet of dough into squares (2x2 cm) and immediately proceed to cooking preventing the dough from drying. The same dough is used for gurza (second course).

Dishes of Cultured Milk

Dishes of fresh and cultured milk, for example, ayran, siuzmya, pendir, etc., are widely spread in Azerbaijani cuisine. These are very tasty and healthy dishes, especially, katyk (homemade yoghurt). They are important for digestion, refresh in hot weather, and are used as seasonings for different dishes and as main ingredients.

This proves the proverb that came to our time throughout the ages, saying "…drink cultured milk, and you will live long".

Pendir (Cheese)

In Azerbaijani cuisine, the precedence is given to the white cheese (pendir). It is made of sheep's, cow's and buffalo milk.

The method of cooking impacts the level of fat,

tastiness, and even its name. Types of cheese differ also in the level of maturity – young cheese (unsalted), medium and ripened ones. Cheese is served with different greens as a casual dish and on the holiday table. They are used for different snacks and at the end of dinner.

Motal (Cheese)

One of the most tasty and original varieties of cheese is motal – cheese, which ripens in a sheep's skin. Depending on the size of the sheep's skin, it can weigh from 5 to 60 kg. After taking the skin off the sheep (it should be thick and have no punctures), add salt to the reverse side of the skin and hang it to dry.

Then turn the skin hairy side up, cut the hair well and comb thoroughly, adding water and washing away small hairs occasionally, until the hair stops shedding.

Then hang the skin to dry. Turn the skin once again hairy side down, thoroughly seal all the holes (tightly tie the legs, sew the back side, so that the air could not penetrate in) and start to fill it in with the salted young cheese through the throat, leaving no empty spaces.

After filling up the skin, seal and put on a board in a cool place. Turn each 4-5 days. Usually, motal is made in summer, and it is ripening until autumn. It is hard to make motal at home.

Desserts, Beverages and Jams

The specific Azerbaijani dessert table represents a colourful image: pahlava, shekerbura, shorgogal, miutakke, irishta pahlavasy, as well as large numbers of halva varieties (over 60 kinds), various types of sugared fruits.

The jam that is prepared not only with traditional for many folk of the world fruits, but also with unripe walnuts, rose petals, figs, cornus fruit, mini-aubergines, watermelon rinds, is also able to add beauty to any table. The taste variety of rose extract sherbets with spearmint, saffron, basil seeds is amazing.

Saffron

A spice acquired from the stamen of the flower of a certain crocus type. Each flower has 3-4 stamen. Saffron is used in preparation of dinners, desserts, pastry, porridges. Saffron is also added to teas. This spice, besides the great aroma, is very beneficial for cardiac system of people.

Normally saffron is brewed, then added to dishes. 0.5 or 1 g or a few stamen, depending on servings, are mixed with 1 or 2 tablespoons of boiling water, covered and infuse for 20-30 minutes.

Dried Fruits – Gah

It is hard to prepare dried fruits in home conditions, it is the business of professionals. It is better to buy them at a market or in store.

Albukhara – dried plum of various kinds (sour and sweet). Sour types are preferable for dinners.
Alycha gahy – dried cherry-plum
Zogal ahtasi – dried cornus fruit w/o seeds

Turshgilas ahtasi – dried cherry w/o seeds
Kishmish – dried grapes, sultana/raisins
Zarindzh – dried barberry
Erik gahy – dried apricots
Sumac – minced barbaris

Different spices and dried herbs necessary for most Azerbaijani dishes.

Sari Kök – cumin
Sumac – minced barbaris
Zira – thyme
Nane gurusi – dried mint
Reihan gurusi – dried basilic
Zenjefil – ginger
Edeva – mix of all spices listed above

All of the mentioned ingredients and spices can be purchased from the following websites:
www.mullako.com
www.healthysupplies.co.uk
www.fruitleather.co.uk
www.realfoods.co.uk
www.onlinefoodgrocery.com
www.efooddepot.com
www.kalamala.com
www.josephsbakery.com
www.amazon.com
www.amazon.co.uk

Product measurements (in grams)

Product	Cup	Tablespoon	Teaspoon
Flour	170	25	10
Rice	250	30	10
Granulated sugar	200	30	10
Powered sugar	180	30	5
Ground nuts	200	30	10
Beans	200	–	–
Sultana	150	20	–
Almonds	200	30	–
Clarified butter	250	20	5
Vegetable oil	150	20	5
Vinegar	–	15	7

Spring

Starters – Salads and Hot and Cold Appetisers

Gabib Nasir ogly Guseynov

Painting: *'Tulips'* (1980s)

Oil on canvas

Inscription on the reverse (in Cyrillic): 'Guseynov Nasir G. og/ Year of birth 1959/ Tulips/60 80' 31 x 23.4 in (78.7 x 59.4 cm)

Provenance: Acquired by the current owner in 1981.

Literature: Bown, M. C., *A Dictionary of Twentieth Century Russian and Soviet Painters 1900 – 1980s*, Izo (1998): 111.

Gabib Nasir ogly Guseynov (b. 1959) studied at Baku Art College until 1973 and was active in Baku.

On the 7th of May 2010 the State Art Museum of Baku opened an exhibition of works of Azerbaijani artists entitled "Unforgettable History" to mark the 65th anniversary of the end of the Great Patriotic War.

V Salad with Cornus Fruit
– Zogal Salaty

Ingredients

◊ 500g mature cornus fruit cherries or 2-3 pomegranates

◊ ½ bunch each of coriander, spring onions, and dill

◊ Salt, to taste

Method

◊ De-stone the cornus fruit and mash them. Finely chop the coriander, green onions, and dill, and mix with the mashed cornus fruit and season with salt.

◊ If you don't have cornus fruit, use the juice of 2-3 pomegranates and their seeds to decorate.

◊ This salad could be served as garnish for any meat, fish, poultry and vegetable dishes and any pilaff.

Liver Paté (My Friend's Recipe)
– *Dostumun Ezmasí*

Ingredients

◊ 500g liver

◊ 3 medium carrots

◊ 2 large onions

◊ Salt

◊ Chilli powder

◊ Olive oil or butter

Method

◊ Boil the carrots. Cut the liver into thin fillets and put into boiling water for 5 minutes, do not throw away the broth from the liver. Cool carrots and liver.

◊ Finely chop the onions and sauté in 2 tablespoons of vegetable oil for 10 minutes, being careful not to brown them. Leave all ingredients to cool.

◊ Mince all the ingredients twice, then add salt and chilli powder to taste, and 20 grams of butter.

◊ Mix and add the liver broth if the paste is still thick. Do not add broth if it is soft.

◊ Put the paste into fridge for 30 minutes. Serve as an appetiser with crackers.

V Salad with Tomatoes and Peppers – *Pomidor-Bibar Salaty*

Ingredients

◊ 2 tomatoes

◊ 1 green pepper

◊ 1 shallot

◊ ½ bunch of coriander

◊ Salt, to taste

Method

◊ Cut the tomatoes into slices, the peppers into circles, the shallot into rings, and finely chop the coriander.

◊ Combine all the ingredients and season with salt (serve without dressing, since salted tomatoes bleed as well).

V Peculiar Salad
– *Bahar Salaty*

Ingredients

◊ ½ head iceberg lettuce

◊ 100g of sour cream

◊ ½ bunch each of coriander and dill

◊ 2 cloves garlic - optional

◊ Salt, to taste

Method

◊ Cut the lettuce into rings, mix with the finely chopped greens and garlic.

◊ Dress with sour cream or organic natural yoghurt, and season with salt.

◊ Salad dressed with organic natural yoghurt is wonderfully light.

V Onion and Vinegar Salad
– *Sirkya-Sogan Salaty*

Ingredients

◊ 2 onions

◊ 4 tablespoons apple cider or grape vinegar

◊ Salt, to taste

Method

◊ Peel the onions and scald with boiling water.

◊ Cut the onions into thin rings, season with salt, sprinkle with vinegar and mix.

◊ Can be served with any hot meat or fish dish and any pilaff.

V Spinach with Eggs and Onions
– *Penjar*

Ingredients

◊ 500 g spinach

◊ 2 eggs

◊ 3 tablespoons any oil

◊ 2 onions

◊ Organic natural yoghurt or garlic yoghurt sauce

◊ Salt, to taste

Method

◊ Wash and cut the spinach into large pieces. Blanch the spinach and immediately strain. Once cooled, squeeze the spinach.

◊ Cut the onions into rings and sauté until golden-brown.

◊ Mix the squeezed spinach with the fried onions.

◊ Beat the eggs, make an omelette, then cut the omelette and put it on top of the spinach.

◊ Add some salt, oil and stew on low heat for 10 minutes.

◊ Serve with the garlic yoghurt sauce, or natural yoghurt.

V Steamed and Browned Asparagus
– *Gulanchar Govurmasy*

Ingredients

◊ 2 bunches asparagus

◊ 1 onion

◊ 2 eggs

◊ 3 tablespoons oil

◊ Salt, to taste

Method

◊ Cut the tips of the asparagus into small pieces (1 cm each), cover with ¼ cup of water and stew for 5-10 minutes until tender. The water should evaporate, but the asparagus should not lose its colour.

◊ Cut the onion into rings, sauté, and mix with the asparagus.

◊ Beat the eggs and make an omelette, using the oil, that was left after sautéing the onion. Before it is completely ready cut it into slices and put on top of the onions and asparagus. Stew everything together for 10 minutes.

◊ Serve hot with vegetables and any salad, or as a cold appetiser.

V Spring Salad – *Yaz Salaty*

Ingredients

◊ 1 onion

◊ ¼ head iceberg lettuce

◊ A few springs coriander or celery

◊ 1 cucumber

◊ 1 tomato

◊ 2-3 radishes

◊ 2 tablespoons each of vinegar and olive oil

◊ Salt and pepper, to taste

Method

◊ Finely chop the lettuce, onions, cucumbers, tomatoes, radishes, and coriander.

◊ Place all the vegetables in layers like a cake, season lightly with salt, and dress with the wine vinegar and olive oil.

◊ Garnish with the fresh herbs.

V Steamed and Browned Purslane
– *Perpetejun Gyzartmasy*

Ingredients

◊ 500 g purslane

◊ 2 onions – cut into rings

◊ 2-3 tablespoons vegetable oil

◊ 1 cup yoghurt or garlic yoghurt sauce

◊ Salt and pepper, to taste

Method

◊ Wash and chop the purslane, then boil it in salted water for 5 minutes, and then strain it. Once cool, slightly squeeze and chop the purslane.

◊ Sauté the onions, mix with the purslane and stew for about 15 minutes.

◊ Serve with the yoghurt.

V Sautéed Quince
– *Haiva Gyzartmasy*

Ingredients

◊ 2 quinces

◊ 4 tablespoons of any oil

◊ Salt, to taste

Method

◊ Slice each quince in 10-12 segments and remove the core. Place evenly into a frying pan; add ¼ glass of water, and stew. When the quince becomes soft and the water has reduced, add 2 tablespoons of oil and sauté.

◊ This can be served as a garnish for poultry or meat, or as a hot appetiser.

V Ratatouille
– *Hiaftabejar*

Ingredients

◊ 1 courgette

◊ 1 aubergine

◊ 3 tomatoes

◊ 1 onion

◊ 1 sweet pepper

◊ 1 chilli or hot pepper

◊ 5 cloves of garlic

◊ 4 tablespoons vegetable oil

◊ Salt, to taste

Method

◊ Finely dice the vegetables and stew in a deep frying pan until the water from the vegetables reduces, then add the oil and sauté.

◊ If serving as a cold snack, stew until the vegetable juice reduces; and if serving as a hot snack or garnish for meat, leave the vegetable juice.

V Herb Casserole
– *Kükü*

Ingredients

◊ 1 bunch each parsley, dill, leafs of spring onions or leek, celery, mint, and coriander

◊ 9 eggs

◊ ½ tablespoon citric acid or lemon juice

◊ 2 tablespoons sumac (spice from the fruit of sumac)

◊ 3 tablespoons melted butter or any vegetable oil

◊ Salt and pepper, to taste

Method

◊ Wash, dry, and finely chop the greens, crack in the eggs, add the citric acid, mix everything well, and season with salt and pepper.

◊ Pour 2 tablespoons of oil or butter into deep, well-heated frying pan, pour in the prepared mixture, and cover with a lid.

◊ After five minutes, when the bottom has set, remove the lid, shake the frying pan from side to side and re-cover. Reduce the heat.

◊ In 15-20 minutes the contents of the frying pan should be cooked through. Then cover the frying pan with a flat plate, and, flipping the frying pan over, put the herb casserole on a plate.

◊ Pour the remaining tablespoon of butter or oil and return the casserole to the frying pan.

◊ Fry for another 5 minutes, uncovered, to brown the reverse side. Cover the frying pan with a plate, flip it over, and put casserole on a plate, sprinkle with sumac, and cut into slices.

◊ Casserole rises up to approximately 2-3 cm.

◊ Serve hot or cold.

◊ Please see the following recipes for variations on this classic dish.

Variation 1:
Herb Casserole with Mackerel
– *Balyg Küküsu*

Ingredients

◊ 200g mackerel (dried or smoked)

◊ 1 bunch each parsley, dill, celery, coriander, leafs of spring onions or leek

◊ 7 eggs

◊ 3-4 tablespoons oil

◊ 1 tablespoon sumac

◊ Lemon juice

◊ Salt and pepper, to taste

Method

◊ Wash, dry, and finely chop the herbs. Beat the eggs with the lemon juice or citric acid and 1 tablespoon of sumac, and add to the herbs.

◊ Boil the fish, flake it into small pieces, pick out bones, mix thoroughly with the prepared herbs in a large bowl, and season with pepper.

◊ Follow the method from the recipe on the previous page.

Variation 2:
Herb Casserole with Chicken
– *Tojuglu Kükü*

Ingredients

◊ 200g boned chicken

◊ 1 bunch each parsley, dill, celery, spring onions, leek, and coriander

◊ 8 eggs

◊ 1 lemon or $\frac{1}{3}$ tablespoon of citric acid

◊ 2 tablespoon sumac

◊ 4 tablespoon olive oil

◊ Salt and pepper, to taste

Method

◊ Finely chop the prepared greens, beat the eggs with the lemon juice or citric acid and 1 tablespoon of sumac, and add to the greens.

◊ Boil and chop the chicken, mix with herbs in a large bowl and season with pepper.

◊ Pour 2 tablespoons of oil and the contents of the bowl into a well heated frying pan, cover with a lid.

◊ After 5 minutes, when the bottom has set, remove the lid, shake the frying pan from side to side for the mixture to slide a little, and re-cover.

◊ In 15-20 minutes the contents of the frying pan will be cooked through. Then cover the frying pan with flat plate, and, flipping the frying pan over, put the kükü on a plate. Pour the remaining oil into the frying pan, heat it, and return o the frying pan.

◊ Fry for an additional 10 minutes, uncovered, to brown the reverse side.

◊ Serve in slices and sprinkle with sumac.

Variation 3:
V   Herb Casserole with Aubergines
– *Badimjan Küküsu*

Ingredients

◊   2 aubergines

◊   2 onions – cut into rings

◊   8 eggs

◊   6 tablespoons vegetable oil

◊   Salt and pepper, to taste

Method

◊   Wash, dice and fry the aubergines in a frying pan in 2 tablespoons of oil until golden brown. Remove from the pan, and sauté the onions on 2 tablespoons of oil.

◊   Thoroughly mix the browned onions and aubergines with the beaten eggs, season with salt and pepper.

◊   Put the whole mixture in the hot frying pan coated with 1 tablespoon of oil, cover with a lid. When the bottom has set shake the frying pan to prevent the mixture from sticking and cover with a lid.

◊   After 15-20 minutes the casserole will be cooked through. Remove the casserole from the pan, add oil and fry the reverse side of the casserole. To serve, cover the pan with a plate and flip the frying pan over.

◊   Serve in slices.

Variation 4:
V Potato Casserole with Leek and Sweet Pepper – *Kartof Kever Küküsu*

Ingredients

◊ 3 sweet peppers

◊ 1 bunch coriander

◊ 1 bunch parsley

◊ 3 leeks

◊ 2 potatoes

◊ 6 eggs

◊ 1 chilli

◊ Salt and pepper to taste

Method

◊ Finely chop all the vegetables and herbs and mix with the eggs.

◊ Put everything into the pre-heated frying pan with melted butter or vegetable oil.

◊ Cover with the lid and cook on medium heat for 15 minutes.

◊ After 15-20 minutes the casserole will be cooked through. Then cover the frying pan with flat plate, and, flipping the frying pan over, put the kükü on a plate. Pour the remaining oil into the frying pan, heat it, and return o the frying pan.

◊ Serve hot or cold.

Soups

Kyamil Ali Abbas ogly Khanlarov

Painting: *'Shusha View of Mirov Dag'* (1976)

Oil on canvas

Signed and dated bottom left (in Cyrillic): '1976 Khanlarov'; inscription on reverse (in Cyrillic): 'Shusha vid mirov dag/oil on canvas size 45 x 60/ Baku 1976/ Kyamil Khanlarov'

17.6 x 23.2 in (44.6 x 59.0 cm)

Provenance: Acquired by the current owner in 2010.

Literature: Bown, M. C., A *Dictionary of Twentieth Century Russian and Soviet Painters 1900 – 1980s*, Izo (1998): 137.

The Fine Arts of the Azerbaijan SSR, Sovyetsky Khudozhnik, Moscow (1978): 87-88. Kyamil Ali-Abbas ogly Khanlarov was born in Baku in 1915. He studied at Baku Art College until 1935 and was later active in Baku.

Khanlarov is said to be the patriarch of painting and it is hard to overestimate the significant contribution he made to the treasury of Azerbaijan's fine arts. He was a highly professional and original artist who told of his love of the land and its people with a distinct style and an emotionally saturated palette.

The best of his works are distinguished by a creative maturity, a harmony of colour, and an all-embracing love for the beauty of his native land. He participated in art exhibitions since 1933, with solo exhibitions in 1961, 1967, 1995 and in 2010, posthumously in Baku. Khanlarov's paintings are held in numerous museums of Azerbaijan, as well as abroad, and the best of them reproduced in important publications. Khanlarov died in 1996.

Meat Noodle Soup
– *Hamrashi*

Ingredients

◊   500 g lamb, veal, or beef

◊   2 onions

◊   2 tablespoons vegetable oil or melted butter

◊   ½ cup mung beans (small pinkish brown soybeans) or small white beans

◊   2 handfuls homemade thin noodles (Arishta) or vermicelli

◊   ½ bunch each coriander and dill

◊   Salt and pepper, to taste

Method

◊   Cut the meat into small pieces and lightly fry together with the chopped onions until meat browns.

◊   Boil the soybeans in 1½ litres of water until tender, mix with the sautéed meat, cook until the meat is ready, add 2 handfuls of noodles, cook for 5 minutes, then add the finely chopped greens.

◊   Serve with a seperate dish of garlic yoghurt sauce (2-3 cloves of garlic mashed in 500 g of natural yoghurt) and fruit vinegar.

◊   Add 1 tablespoon of sauce or 1 teaspoon of vinegar (also with mashed garlic) into each serving.

V Soup with Hart's-Tongue Fern
– *Evelik Shorbasy*

Ingredients

◊ ½ pigtail hart's-tongue fern

◊ 2 potatoes

◊ 1 onion

◊ 4-5 cloves garlic

◊ 2 tablespoons melted butter or vegetable oil

◊ 1 egg

◊ 1 teaspoon flour

◊ 1 bunch parsley

◊ 100 g sour cream

◊ Salt and pepper, to taste

Method

◊ Drop the hart's-tongue fern into 1½ litres of cold water and cook for 10-15 minutes, then remove from the water.

◊ Cut the potato into 4 pieces and drop it in the broth together with the mashed garlic and chopped pre-cooked hart's-tongue fern. While the potatoes are cooking, fry the finely chopped onion, and add to the broth.

◊ When the potatoes are ready, mix the egg with the flour and ½ cup of water until smooth and pour into the boiling soup stirring it at a steady pace. Once thick, turn off the heat and add the finely chopped parsley.

◊ Serve with sour cream. This dish can also be cooked with chicken or meat broth.

V Light Vegetable Soup with Herbs and Fruit – *Turshulu Suyug*

Ingredients

◊ 2 carrots

◊ 1-2 sweet peppers

◊ 2 onions

◊ 100 g rice

◊ 2 tablespoons oil

◊ 1 bunch each coriander, spring onions or leek, celery, and parsley

◊ 10-15 cherry plums or sour yellow plums or 1 lemon

◊ Quince (seasonally)

◊ Salt and pepper, to taste

Method

◊ Finely chop the onions, peppers and carrots, and sauté them in oil.

◊ Boil the rice and cherry plums in 2 litres of water until the rice is par-cooked, then add all the finely chopped fresh greens, and chopped quince. Cook until the rice is tender and then add the sautéed vegetables.

◊ Season with salt and pepper, add lemon juice (or a pinch of citric acid), and 1 teaspoon of cherry plum sauce, or fresh cherry plums (seasonally).

◊ The soup should be thick. The same soup can be cooked with chicken or meat broth.

Offal Dishes

Mikail Gusein ogly Abdullaev

Painting: *'Landscape/Quba'* (1984)

Oil on canvas

Signed bottom right 'M. Abdullaev' (in Cyrillic), inscription on reverse (in Latin script): 'Abdullahi – Lanshaft /Quba/'

25 x 38.1 in (63.5 x 96.8 cm)

Provenance: Gift to the current owner from the artist in 1985

Literature: Bown, M. C., *A Dictionary of Twentieth Century Russian and Soviet Painters 1900 – 1980s*, Izo (1998): 3.

Bown, M. C., *Socialist Realist Painting*, Yale University Press (1998): 266 - 268, 290, 358 and 307.

The Fine Arts of the Azerbaijan SSR, Sovyetsky Khudozhnik, Moscow (1978): 4-8.

Mikail Gusein ogly Abdullaev (1921-2007) studied at the Azerbaijan Art College (1935-39) and the Surikov Art Institute in Moscow (1939-49) under S.V.Gerasimov. Abdullaev was declared an honoured Artist of Azerbaijan SSR (1955), the People's Artist of the USSR (1963), and was later made a member of the Academy of Arts (1988) and a recipient of the Lenin Award (1959). The landscape painting displayed in this book is a depiction of the mountain Shah-Dag (the highest mountain in the Great Caucasus 4243m) near the city of Quba, Azerbaijan.

Lamb or Veal Liver Paté
– *Bagyrbeyin*

Ingredients

◊ 500 g liver (lamb, veal or calf)

◊ 300 g sheep tail fat

◊ 2 onion heads

◊ Salt and pepper, to taste

Method

◊ Boil the liver, tail fat and onion until ready.

◊ Run everything through a meat grinder, and season with salt and pepper to taste

◊ Add the remaining broth, so that the mass density is of a very thick sour cream, and serve.

◊ Serve as an appetiser, or as an accompaniment to one of the types of pilaff (chuyutli ash, parchadeshema ash). Serve with salads, fresh greens and marinades.

Main Dishes - Meat

Sattar Bakhul ogly Bakhlul-Zade

Painting: '*Self Portrait*' (1968)

Charcoal on paper

Not signed

43.3 x 41.3 in (110 x 105 cm)

Provenance: Acquired by the current owner in 2002 through the Baku Centre of Art.

Literature: Bown, M. C., *A Dictionary of Twentieth Century Russian and Soviet Painters 1900 – 1980s*, Izo (1998):22.

The Fine Arts of the Azerbaijan SSR, Sovyetsky Khudozhnik, Moscow (1978): 22 – 25.

Sattar Bakhlul ogly Bakhlul-Zade (1909-1974) was born in Amiradjan, a village near Baku. He was named the People's Artist of Azerbaijan SSR, and granted the National Azerbaijan SSR award. His artistic education began in 1933 in the Drawing Department at the Moscow Surikov Fine Arts Institute, where he studied under Vladimir Favorsky. During summer workshops in the Crimea, the Russian painter Marc Chagall saw some of Bakhlul-Zade's sketches and suggested that he transfer to the Institute's Painting Department.

Bakhlul-Zade began exhibiting in 1940. His solo exhibitions include: Baku (1955, 1960, 1974), Yerevan (1956), Tbilisi (1956), Moscow (1965, 1973), and the National Gallery in Prague (1964/6). After the exhibition in Prague five of his works were selected for the museum's collection.

Stewed Meat and Herbs
– *Siabzi Govurma*

Ingredients

◊ 1 kg lamb (fillet, brisket meat or shoulder)

◊ 3 onions

◊ Parsley, celery, mint, tarragon, chives (a kind of spring onion) or the green of 2 leeks, 1 bunch each

◊ 10-15 fresh or dried cherry plums, lemon acid (4 pinches), sour yellow plums or 3 tablespoons of grape juice or lemon juice

◊ 3 tablespoons oil or mutton fat

◊ Salt and pepper, to taste

Method

◊ Cut the meat into small pieces, add ½ a glass of water, cover with the lid, and stew. Finely chop two onions and sauté with the meat until it is cooked.

◊ Sauté one onion in oil and when the meat is ready, put it in a saucepan with the cherry plums.

◊ Chop the herbs into 2.5 cm pieces. Sauté in oil separately for 5-10 minutes, stirring occasionally, then put in a saucepan and add the dissolved citric acid and stew for another 10-15 minutes.

◊ Serve with pickles and bread or as a garnish for pilaff.

Oven Baked Leg of Lamb or Mutton Loins – *Guzu Sobada*

Ingredients

◊ 2-4 mutton loins or one large leg of lamb

◊ 1 tablespoon turmeric

◊ 2 tablespoons olive oil

◊ Salt, to taste

Method

◊ Coat the mutton loins with oil, add a little salt, sprinkle turmeric thickly, then wrap in aluminium foil and place in the hot oven.

◊ Add 2 cups of water. Bake at 200°C for 2–3 hours.

◊ Serve with baked tomatoes, fried quince or a baked potato.

Variation:
Oven Baked Caramelized Meat – *Guzu Injil Shiriasinde*

Ingredients

◊ 1 leg lamb

◊ Sweet jam syrup (or fresh figs)

Method

◊ Put the leg of lamb onto the foil and coat both sides with vegetable oil and the sweet jam syrup. Or use halved fresh figs.

◊ Wrap in foil and put into a hot oven (250°C) for 4–5 hours. Serve with green salad, roasted potatoes and roasted quince fruit.

Dolma

There is a series of dishes called "dolma", meaning "stuffed". This reflects the method of its preparation: grapes and cabbage leaves, aubergines, peppers, tomatoes, pumpkin are stuffed with meat, chicken, vegetable stuffing, and in some beach regions – with fish stuffing. Dolma are interesting, healthy and tasty dishes.

Ingredients

Option 1

◊ 1½ kg fresh grapes leaves per 3-litre glass jar or marinated grape leaves

◊ 2 bunches dill

◊ Salt, to taste

Option 2

Option 3

Preparing vine leaves for dolma

◊ To preserve the leaves for the use in winter, they should be salted. Pour the leaves with water in a deep vessel, and leave for 2-3 hours. Then wash, and, gathering in groups of 15-20, stack them the front side down, add a pinch of salt and put in the bottom of the glass jar. Proceed until the jar is filled, occasionally introducing some dill. Cover all the upper leaves with dill and add enough salted water (3 tablespoons of salt per 1 litre of water). Close with a plastic lid and put the jar in a bowl, so that in the process the water does not flow out on the floor. Occasionally add salted water, so that the leaves do not dry. After fermentation add salted water once again and put in a cool place. Wash well and pour with boiling water before use.

◊ Take a plastic bottle (1 litre), for example a leftover drinks bottle, and fill it with with leaves wrapped in rolls. Fill the bottle thoroughly and seal the lid. In 2-3 days open the lid slightly to let out a little air, then re-seal. Repeat this process 2-3 times. Before use, cut the bottle throat with a knife and remove the leaves. Rinse with boiling water, squeeze slightly and stuff them with the stunning.

◊ You can store the leaves by portions, wrapping them in paper and putting in a plastic bag in a freezer. Unfrozen, wash, scald and wrap a dolma before use.

◊ Mulberry leaves and wild grapes leaves can be used instead of grapes leaves. And this, for sure, adds a different zest to a dish. Young, thin and not shaggy leaves are used for the preparation of dolma.

Stuffed Vine Leaves with Meat
– *Yarpag Dolmasy*

Ingredients

◊   1 kg lamb, (veal or beef)

◊   2 large onions

◊   1 bunch each of parsley, dill, spring onions, and mint (if there is no fresh mint, you can use dried)

◊   100 g rice

◊   300 g grapes leaves

◊   200 g dried cherry plums (or fresh, or 50 g of its extract) or 2-3 pinches of citric juice

◊   Natural yoghurt with or without crushed garlic

◊   Salt and pepper, to taste

Method

◊   Prepare a stuffing with the lamb and onions, add the finely chopped greens and washed rice, black ground pepper, citric acid, salt and turmeric. Stir all the ingredients thoroughly.

◊   Wash the grape leaves beforehand to remove the redundant salt. Stuff each leaf with the stuffing and make a kind of parcel, then place them in the saucepan.

◊   Then add cherry plums or citric acid to the stuffing. Add 1 cup of water, cover with a lid and boil for 1 hour until cooked. If the water reduces, add another ½ cup.

◊   Use a copper, teflon or aluminium saucepan. Line the saucepan with meat bones or grape leaves to prevent it from burning.

◊   Serve and dress with the yoghurt sauce.

Main Dishes - Poultry

Stewed Chicken with Leeks and Lemon – *Toyug-Límon Buglamasy*

Ingredients

◊ 2 small poussins or 1 chicken

◊ 3 small lemons, halved

◊ 3 medium leeks

◊ Salt and pepper, to taste

Method

◊ Divide the chicken into several parts, finely chop leeks, add the lemons without removing the peel.

◊ Stew all the ingredients together for 45 minutes. Serve with any green salad.

Chicken Stew with Tomatoes
– *Pomidor Toyug Chygyrtmasy*

Ingredients

◊   1 whole chicken

◊   5 tomatoes

◊   3 onion heads

◊   2 eggs

◊   2 tablespoons oil or butter

◊   Salt, pepper – optional

Method

◊   Cut the chicken into pieces, mix with the chopped onion, add salt, 1 cup of water and the oil to the pan, stew and lightly sautée under a lid.

◊   Rub the tomatoes through a sieve and add to the pan, stew for 10–15 minutes, then add the beaten eggs. Cover with the lid to cook the eggs.

◊   Serve with any salads.

Quails with Eggs and Onions
– Bildirchin Chygyrtmasy

Ingredients

◊ 1–2 quails per serving

◊ 10 quail eggs

◊ 2 onion heads

Method

◊ Stew the quails with the chopped onion and 1 cup of water and cook until the quails are ready.

◊ Prepare an omelette with the eggs.

◊ When cooked, add pomegranate or lemon juice (or citric acid) and sprinkle with sumac, place the omelette on top.

Roast Chicken with Quince
– *Haivaly Toyug Sobada*

Ingredients

◊ 1 whole chicken

◊ 1 or 2 quince fruits (or plums and apples)

◊ 1 teaspoon turmeric

◊ 1 tablespoon olive oil

◊ Salt – optional

Method

◊ Wash the chicken, cover it with turmeric on the outside and inside, add salt, cut the quinces (apples) into slices and stuff the chicken, then sew it up. Wrap in foil and place in the pre-heated oven.

◊ Bake for 1 hour at 200°C, then open the foil and cook for a further 5 minutes. Pour the juice from the quinces (apples) over the chicken. Place the stewed fruits on the dish beside the chicken.

◊ The same recipe may be used for preparing turkey, guinea fowl, or duck. The dish is better when prepared with quince.

Hot Chicken Wings
– *Toyug Ganadlary Buglamasy*

Ingredients

◊ 1 kg chicken wings

◊ 3 tablespoons tomato paste

◊ 2 tablespoons red pepper or chilli

◊ 3 tablespoons olive oil

◊ Salt – optional

Method

◊ Mix the chicken wings with salt and stew for 10 minutes in a pan.

◊ Prepare a sauce with tomato paste and pepper (add water to reach the density of a watery sour cream) and pour it over the wings.

◊ Stew under a lid for another 10 minutes, pour over the oil and stew for a further 5 minutes.

◊ Once cooked, pour the hot sauce over the wings and serve.

◊ Serve hot or cold.

Main Dishes - Fish

Nadir Gambar ogly Abdurakhmanov

Painting: 'Youth' (undated)

Oil on canvas

Inscription on the reverse (in Cryillic): 'N. Abdurakhmanov Youth 73 x 92 cm'

28.7 x 36.2 in (73.0 x 92.0 cm)

Provenance: Acquired by the current owner in 1998.

Literature: Bown, M. C., *A Dictionary of Twentieth Century Russian and Soviet Painters 1900 – 1980s*, Izo (1998): 4.

The Fine Arts of the Azerbaijan SSR, Sovyetsky Khudozhnik, Moscow (1978): 11 -13.

Nadir Gambar ogly Abdurakhmanov (1925-2008) was born in Lachin, Azerbaijan. He studied at the Repin Institute between 1947 and 1953 and then settled in Baku, Azerbaijan, beginning to exhibit in 1946. He taught at Baku Art College from 1954 to 1962 and was a chairman of the Azerbaijan Artists' Union between 1961 and 1970. His important shows include the 'All-Union Art Exhibition', put on in Moscow in 1952 and 1955.

Abdurakhmanov specialized in thematic paintings and landscapes; the painting Youth shown here is a wonderful example of his preferred technique.

Zander Stuffed with Almonds and Onions – *Suf Liaviangi*

Ingredients

◊ 1 large zander

◊ 200 g walnuts or almonds (shelled)

◊ 2 onion heads

◊ 2 tablespoons narsharab or cherry-plum sauce

◊ Salt – optional

Method

◊ Wash and dry the fish. Run the onions and nuts through a meat grinder, add salt and mix thoroughly with the cherry-plum sauce or narsharab.

◊ Stuff the belly of the fish with the filling and sew it up.

◊ Place the fish on a tray and smear with the cherry-plum sauce or sour lavash (previously soaked cherry-plum lavash).

◊ Pour 1 cup of water and put into a preheated oven.

◊ Bake at 180°C until the top is crispy.

◊ Serve hot with salads and marinades.

Main Dishes - Pilaffs

Togrul Farman ogly Narimanbekov

Painting: *'Composition Tenderness'* (1977)

Mixed media on composite board
27.5 x 39.2 in (69.9 x 99.6 cm)

Provenance: Acquired by the current owner in 2010.

Literature: Bown, M. C., *A Dictionary of Twentieth Century Russian and Soviet Painters 1900 – 1980s*, Izo (1998): 218.

The Fine Arts of the Azerbaijan SSR, Sovyetsky Khudozhnik, Moscow (1978): 59 -62.

Togrul Farman ogly Narimanbekov was born in Baku in 1930. He is the honoured artist of the Azerbaijan SSR, laureate of the Azerbaijan State Prize and laureate of the Azerbaijan Lenin Comsomol prize. Narimanbekov studied at the Baku Art College until 1950. In 1955 he graduated from the Vilnyus Art Institute. Narimanbekov began exhibiting around 1952. His personal exhibitions include: Baku, 1961, 1965, 1975; Moscow, 1967, 1972; Vilnyus, 1972; Volgograd, 1973; Prague, 1965; Wroclaw, Warsaw, Sopot, 1973; and Lviv, 1975. Narimanbekov was also vice-president of the Committee for Solidarity of Asia and Africa (1973) and a member of the Peace Committee (1981). He died in Paris in 2013.

V Filtered Pilaff
– *Siuzmya Ash*

This type of pilaff is served with various side dishes, or with a fruit garnish (Hurush).

Ingredients

◊ 3 cups basmati rice

◊ 0.5 g saffron

◊ ½ teaspoon cumin and zira

◊ 50-100 g butter or clarified butter

◊ Salt – optional

Method

◊ Pour the saffron into one tablespoon of boiled water and let it infuse. The rice should be soaked overnight in well salted water. Before cooking, rinse the rice thoroughly, boil in salted water for 5-7 minutes until par-cooked (The rice should still be hard inside) and strain. Cooked this way, the rice does not stick into lumps.

◊ Put 1 tablespoon of oil into a large pot or a pan with wide bottom. Prepare a kazmag and place it on the bottom of the pan.

◊ Pour the rice into a slope and spread it with a skimmer without shaking, sprinkle it with saffron, cumin or zira and close it tightly with a lid rolled into a cotton tissue or towel.

◊ Put it on a low heat to cook for 40 min. When the rice is ready, it opens up and yields a delicious aroma. Then pour the melted butter and let it cook using this absorbtion methiod for an additional 10-15 minutes and serve on an oval dish in a nice slope.

◊ *Please see the Practical Guide section at the front of this book for how to prepare Filtered Pilaff with Kazmag Crust (page 21).*

V Hurush

A common side dish for all types of filtered pilaff (siuzmya ash) is called Hurush.

Ingredients

◊ 200 g sultanas or raisins

◊ 100 g dried apricots

◊ Pomegranate seeds (2 fruit)

◊ 3-4 onion heads

◊ 200/300 g chestnuts – boiled and peeled

◊ Olive oil or melted butter

Method

◊ Sauté the onions until browned, add the raisins, dried apricots and chestnuts, add ¼ cup of water and stew them for 10-15 minutes (let the water boil down). When ready, serve and decorate with fresh pomegranate seeds.

◊ The pilaff is served in the shape of a slope and the garnished with the hurush. Other side dishes to accompany this are described in the section for meat and chicken dishes: siuzmya ash with roasted aubergines, siuzmya ash with musamba, siuzmya ash with govurma, siuzmya ash with tas kebab, siuzmya ash with quail, siuzmya ash with chicken chygyrtma.

V Filtered Pilaff with Dill
– *Chuyutli Ash*

Ingredients

◊ 4 cups rice – soaked overnight

◊ 1 kg lamb or beef (brisket, shoulder blade)

◊ 2 large bunches of dill

◊ 0.5 g saffron

◊ 4 tablespoons clarified butter

◊ 1 pomegranate

◊ Salt and pepper – optional

Method

◊ Cut the meat into large pieces and boil. Let the meat cool down. Add salt and pepper and wrap in a cheesecloth.

◊ Chop the dill.

◊ Rinse the rice and boil in salty water for 5-7 minutes until half-cooked and strain. Mix with the dill.

◊ Prepare a kazmag (see page 21), place it on the bottom of the pot onto the oil, pour on a layer of the rice (1 cm thick) and lay down the meat. Cover it with the remaining rice in a slope. Close the pot with a lid wrapped in a cotton tissue.

◊ Put the rice on a low heat to cook using the absorbtion method for 40 min. Then pour warm oil over it and cook for 10-15 more minutes.

◊ Serve the rice and meat and sprinkle with pomegranate seeds. This pilaff is generally prepared during the Spring.

Pilaff with Steamed Meat Cooked under Rice – *Parcha-Dioshiamya Ash*

Ingredients

◊ 4 cups rice – soaked overnight

◊ 1 kg lamb or beef (brisket)

◊ 2 onion heads

◊ 0.5 g saffron

◊ ½ teaspoons cumin or zira

◊ 4 tablespoons butter

◊ Salt and pepper – to taste

Method

◊ Boil the meat, add salt, pepper and wrap it into cheesecloth.

◊ Mix the saffron with 2 tablespoons of boiling water and let it infuse.

◊ Rinse the rice and boil in salty water for 5-7 minutes until half-cooked and strain.

◊ Prepare a kazmag (see page 21), place it on the bottom of the pot onto the oil. Pour a layer of rice 1 cm thick and lay down the meat, cover it with the remaining rice in a slope, sprinkle cumin or zira, pour the saffron and tightly close the pot with a lid wrapped in a cotton tissue, then put it on a low heat to cook for 40 min, then pour over the warm butter and cook for a further 10 minutes.

◊ Put the rice on a dish trying to manage the rice with saffron on the top, place the meat around the rice.

◊ Serve with marinades and green salads with vinegar.

◊ *Please see the Practical Guide section at the front of this book for how to prepare Filtered Pilaff with Kazmag Crust (page 21).*

Dough Dishes

Rasim Ganifa ogly Babayev

Painting: *'Spring'* (1996)

Oil on canvas

Signed bottom right: 'Rasim'; inscription on the reverse:' Rasim Hanifa oglu, 'Bahar', yagli boya. 1996, 90x70'

27.6 x 35.4 in (70.0 x 90.0 cm)

Provenance: Acquired by the current owner in 2012 from a private collection.

Literature: Bown, M. C., *A Dictionary of Twentieth Century Russian and Soviet Painters 1900 – 1980s*, Izo (1998): 21.

The Fine Arts of the Azerbaijan SSR, Sovyetsky Khudozhnik, Moscow (1978): 18-20.

The painter Rasim Ganifa ogly Babayev (1927-2007) was born in Baku. In 1949 he graduated from the Azerbaijan State Art School named after Azimzade in Baku. In 1955 he graduated from the Moscow Surikov Institute, Faculty of Painting. In 1964, Babayev was made an Honoured Artist of Azerbaijan.

V Very Thin Dough with Steamed Herbs – *Gey Kutaby*

Ingredients

◊   1 kg flour

◊   1 egg

◊   2 cups water

◊   Salt – optional

Stuffing:

◊   1 bunch each of coriander, dill, celery, and spinach

◊   100 g butter

◊   Vegetable oil

◊   1 onion head

◊   Salt, pepper– optional

Method

◊   Prepare a stiff dough with flour, egg, water, salt, and cover it with a towel.

◊   Divide the dough into 5 cm balls, and roll them into thin disks of 15 cm in diameter.

◊   Wash and chop the herbs. Chop the onion and sauté lightly in vegetable oil. Add salt and pepper. Mix the herbs with the onion and lightly sauté together under a lid.

◊   Put a little of the stuffing on one half of the disk of dough. Cover it with the second half and pinch the edges.

◊   Bake on a non-stick turned over pan on both sides. When ready put them on a dish and smear with butter.

◊   Serve stacked on a plate.

Desserts, Jams and Beverages

Lyatif Abdul Bagi ogly Feizullaev

Painting: *'An Old Part of the Countryside'* (1963)

Oil on canvas

29.4 x 46.9 in (74.7 x 119.1 cm)

Provenance: Acquired by the current owner in 1998.

Literature: Bown, M. C., *A Dictionary of Twentieth Century Russian and Soviet Painters 1900 – 1980s*, Izo (1998): 85.

The Fine Arts of the Azerbaijan SSR, Sovyetsky Khudozhnik, Moscow (1978): 84 – 85.

The painter Lyatif Abdul Bagi ogly Feizullaev (1918-1980s) was born in Baku. He is an honoured Artist of Azerbaijan SSR. Feizullaev graduated from the Surikov Art Institute in Moscow in 1949. He has participated in numerous exhibitions since 1940. Feizullaev's personal exhibitions in Baku took place in 1961 and 1969, and in Moscow in 1973. His works are presented in Azerbaijan State Museum of Art, Lankaran State Art Gallery, in Vajiha Samadova gallery, in private galleries.

V Dense Buttery Confection with Rose Water – *Ter Halva*

Ingredients

◊ 250 g butter or clarified butter

◊ Flour – as much as it takes

◊ 1 litre water

◊ 500 ml saffron infusion

◊ ¾ cup rose water or 1 teaspoon ground ginger or cinnamon

◊ 500 g granulated sugar

Method

◊ To prepare the syrup, add water to the sugar and the saffron infusion (0.5 g for 2 tablespoons of hot water). Add the rose water (giulab), and boil it.

◊ Melt the butter in a pan and fry the flour.

◊ Pour the boiling syrup on the fried flour, keep on a heat and stir to prevent lumps.

◊ Put on dessert plates and make patterns. If no rose water is available, garnish with the ground ginger or cinnamon.

V Rose Petal Jam
– *Gül Miuryabbyasi*

Ingredients

◊ 100 g petals of tea rose or briar flowers

◊ 1 kg granulated sugar

◊ 1 litre water

◊ 1 pinch citric acid

Method

◊ Prepare the sugar syrup and boil it.

◊ Add the rose petals into the syrup and boil until ready (drip the syrup on the back of a spoon) – if it is thick and does not spread too much, then it is safe to remove from heat.

◊ Add a pinch of citric acid, stir and pour into jars.

◊ Remove the foam from the jam when boiling.

V Sweet Almond Cardamon Pastry – *Shekerbura*

Ingredients

◊ 1 kg almonds or hazelnuts

◊ 1 kg granulated sugar

◊ 8-10 cardamon pods

◊ 2 kg flour

◊ 10 egg yolks

◊ 750 g sour cream

◊ 1 cup milk

◊ 10 g yeast

Method

◊ Soak the yeast in ⅓ cup of milk, add 1 tablespoon of granulated sugar and add the flour. Add the remaining milk and softened butter. Knead the dough and leave in a warm place for 30 minutes. Grind the nuts and cardamon, and mix with granulated sugar.

◊ Prepare round flapjacks from the dough (the size of a tea rosette), put the stuffing on them, make a decorative seam, decorate the top with patterns (for example herringbone – with tweezers), and place in the pre-heated oven. Bake at 180°C for 30-40 minutes.

V Sweet Pastry Parcels filled with Nuts and Spices – *Biukme*

Ingredients

◊ 250 g sour cream

◊ 4 cups of flour

◊ 2 egg yolks

◊ 100 g butter

◊ 3 g each coriander seeds and cumin

◊ 1 cup granulated sugar

◊ 2 cups shelled walnuts or almonds

◊ 100 g shelled pistachios

Method

◊ Beat the sour cream with a yolk and add butter, salt and flour. Knead into a dough.

◊ For the stuffing: ground the nuts, cumin and coriander seeds and mix with the granulated sugar.

◊ Cut the pistachios into smaller pieces.

◊ Roll the dough to a thickness of 2-3mm and cut into a circle using a saucepan. Place the stuffing on half of the circle, roll the dough up and fold. Brush the top with egg yolk and sprinkle with pistachios.

◊ Bake at 180°c.

◊ Biukme can be triangle shaped too. To do this cut a diamond shape out of the dough before placing the stuffing and then pinching the opposite corners of the diamond together.

V Pahlava with Walnuts or Almonds
– *Pahlava*

Ingredients

◊ 1½ kg shelled nuts

◊ 500 g butter

◊ 2 eggs

◊ 800 g flour

◊ 1½ kg granulated sugar

◊ 200 g rose water

◊ 2 g saffron

◊ 600 ml water

◊ 50 g hash-hash
(white poppy seeds)

◊ 50 g pistachios (or almonds)

◊ Salt – optional

Method

◊ Put two egg yolks, 100 g of softened butter, and a pinch of salt into the flour and knead the dough. Divide it into 10 parts. Peel the nuts and put them into boiling water, then dry and grind them, mixing them with 500 g of granulated sugar. Divide the stuffing into 7 parts.

◊ Generously smear the tray with oil/butter.

◊ Roll one part of the dough into a thin layer, cover the whole bottom of the tray. Stick the edges to the sides of the tray, smear with butter, add one more layer of rolled dough, smear with butter again, add a layer of nuts and repeat.

◊ Between the last layers of dough (9 and 10) as with the first layers 1 and 2 should be only the butter. Stick the edges thoroughly and press with your hands.

◊ Cut the pahlava into diamond shapes.

◊ Smear the whole surface with the saffron infusion using a brush, sprinkle the corners of diamonds with hash-hash (white poppy) and place a half of pistachio (or almond) in the middle of each diamond.

◊ Bake at 180°C for one hour (after the tray warms up, pour the remaining butter over the pahlava). Prepare a syrup with the granulated sugar and water and add rose water. Take the ready pahlava out of the oven and pour the hot syrup over it.

◊ After 12 hours put pahlava in a saucepan with a lid. Pahlava can be stored for 10-15 days.

V Spicy Oven-Baked Buns
– *Shorgogal*

Ingredients

For dough:
◊   1½ kg flour

◊   30 g yeast

◊   500 g milk

◊   100 g butter

◊   6 egg yolks

◊   3 tablespoons granulated sugar

◊   Salt – optional

For the stuffing:
◊   500 g flour

◊   1 teaspoon each of – anise, cumin, cinnamon, black pepper

◊   2 teaspoons each turmeric and salt

◊   3 tablespoons clarified butter

Separately:
◊   1½ kg butter

◊   100 g poppy

◊   1 egg

Method

◊   Prepare the pre-dough by dissolving the yeast in warm milk and add 750 g of flour), and put in a warm place for 4 hours.

◊   As soon as the pre-dough increases in size, add the warm butter, sugar, and mix it. Add the yolks, salt and granulated sugar, and mix. Then and add the remaining flour. Mix thoroughly to reach a homogenous mass and put in a warm place for 1 – 1.5 hours.

◊   For the stuffing: pound the cumin and fry it, add the other spices and clarified butter, then mix together and fry for 5 minutes. Divide the ready dough into 10 parts, roll each part into thin layers, generously smear each layer with butter and stack with another layer of the dough.

◊   Cut the multi-layered dough into 6-7 cm thick strips. Divide each strip into 10 parts, then curl each part into a spiral, make an opening in the centre, squash into a flapjack approximately the size of your palm, smear with the beaten egg, sprinkle with poppy, place on a tray, cover with a towel and let them rest for 10-15 minutes.

◊   Put the tray in a preheated oven. Bake at 180°C for 30-40 mins. Shorgogal can be stored in a pot for a long time, covered with a lid.

V Drinks

Sweet Refreshing Drink with Saffron – *Zefferan Sherbeti*

Ingredients

◊ 0.5 g saffron
◊ 200 g granulated sugar
◊ 1 litre water

Method

◊ Pour the hot syrup over the saffron.
◊ Serve cold.
◊ Please see more variations below.

Sweet Refreshing Drink with Lemon Peels – *Lumu Sherbeti*

Ingredients

◊ Peel of 5-6 lemons
◊ 200g granulated sugar
◊ 2 litres water

Method

◊ Chop the lemon peel and pour over the hot syrup.
◊ Serve cold with dinner.

Sweet Refreshing Drink with Sumac – *Sumac Sherbeti*

Ingredients

◊ 100 g sumac
◊ 200 g granulated sugar
◊ 1½ litres water

Method

◊ Pour the hot syrup over the sumac.
◊ Serve cold.

Sweet Refreshing Drink with Spearmint – *Nane Sherbeti*

Ingredients

◊ 1 bunch spearmint
◊ 200 g granulated sugar
◊ 1½ litres water

Method

◊ Wash the spearmint, cut the leaves, pour with hot syrup.
◊ Serve cold.

Sweet Refreshing Drink with Rose Petals – *Gul Sherbeti*

Ingredients

◊ 50 g tea rose petals
◊ 200 g granulated sugar
◊ 1½ litres water
◊ 1 pinch citric acid

Method

◊ Pour the hot syrup over the rose petals, add a pinch of citric acid.
◊ Serve cold.

Summer

Starters – Salads and Hot and Cold Appetisers

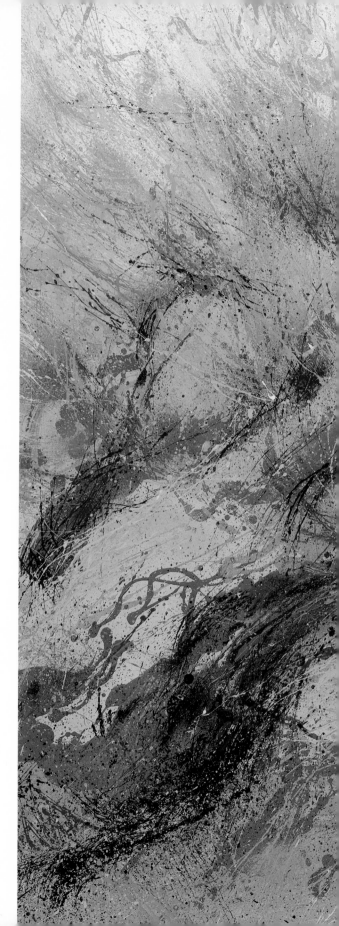

Shakhpalank Abbas ogly Mamedov

Painting: *'Summer'* (1988)

Oil on canvas

Inscription on reverse (in Cryllic): 'Mamedov Shakhpalank Abass og/ 1959 D.oB./ 'Summer' oil on canvas size 100 120 cm/ 1988'

39.2 x 46.0 in (99.6 x 116.8 cm)

Provenance: Acquired by the current owner from the painter in 1988.

Literature: Bown, M. C., *A Dictionary of Twentieth Century Russian and Soviet Painters 1900 – 1980s*, Izo (1998): 199.

Painter Shakhpalank Abbas ogly Mamedov was born in 1959 and is active in Baku, Azerbaijan.

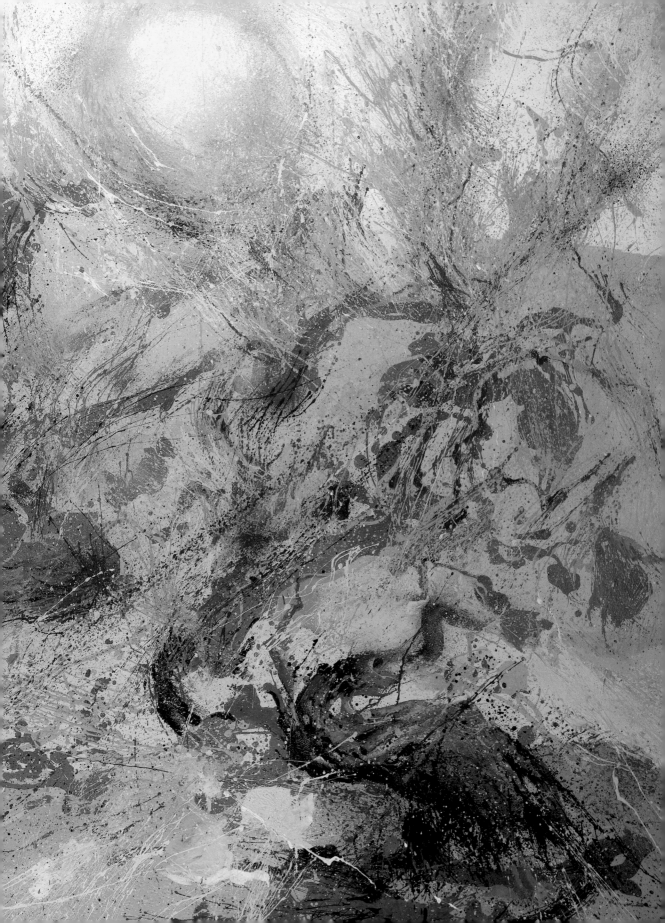

V Salad with Tomatoes and Coriander – *Pomidor – Keshnish Salaty*

Ingredients

◊ 2 tomatoes

◊ ½ bunch each coriander, dill, and tarragon

◊ 2 sweet peppers

◊ 3-4 leafs spring onions

◊ 100 g sour cream (you can use low fat sour cream or organic natural yoghurt)

◊ Walnuts or almonds

◊ Salt and pepper, to taste

Method

◊ Cut the tomatoes into slices. Finely chop the dill, coriander, and spring onions. Cut the sweet peppers into rings.

◊ Mix with the sour cream, decorate with any herbs, and season with salt and pepper. Herbs in all the salads are interchangeable, but mainly coriander and estragon impart piquancy.

◊ You can add either crushed walnuts or almonds to decorate.

Puff pastry with Feta Cheese
– *Pendir Chudusu*

Ingredients

◊ Puff pastry

◊ 1 large bunch coriander

◊ Feta cheese

◊ 2 egg yolks

◊ Mint or basil

Method

◊ Roll out the dough, cut it into squares (6x6), and put the cheese with finely chopped greens in the middle. Close it into a parcel and brush each one with egg yolk. Preheat the oven and bake for 20 minutes.

◊ Alternatively, the same pastry can be made with spinach and leeks or mince meat.

V Grilled Aubergine Paté
– *Mangalda Hazyrlanmysh Badymjan Ezmesi*

Ingredients

◊   1 bunch coriander

◊   ½ bunch dill

◊   3 aubergines

◊   2 tablespoons vegetable oil

◊   Salt and pepper, to taste

Method

◊   Roast the whole aubergines on the grill. Peel them and cut in very small pieces. Wash, dry and chop the herbs. Add the grilled aubergines, mix all together, and season with salt.

◊   Add olive oil if desired.

◊   Serve with meat or fish, or as a cold starter.

V Salad with Feta and Tomatoes
– *Pendir Pomidor Salaty*

Ingredients

◊ 2 tomatoes

◊ 100 g feta cheese or sheep's milk cheese

◊ ½ bunch purple basil, or coriander each

Method

◊ Cut the tomatoes across into circles, and sprinkle with the cheese and finely chopped basil or coriander.

◊ There is no need to add salt, since feta or sheep's milk cheese is sufficiently salty.

V Salad with Sour Cherries
– *Turshgilas Salaty*

Ingredients

◊   500 g pitted fresh or frozen sour cherries (there is a variety to choose from such as Early Richmond or Montmorency)

◊   1 bunch each coriander and basil

◊   ½ bunch mint

◊   1 onion

◊   Salt, to taste

Method

◊   De-stone cherries, and mash lightly. (You can use frozen cherries in winter.)

◊   Cut the onion into rings, cover it with mashed cherries, and season with salt.

◊   Chop the greens and combine all the ingredients.

◊   Serve as a side dish with any hot meat or fish dish, or any pilaff.

V Fried Rosemary Potatoes
– *Myarzyali Kartof*

Ingredients

◊ 6-8 potatoes

◊ 3 tablespoons any oil
or 100g sheep tail fat

◊ Dry or fresh rosemary

◊ Salt and pepper, to taste

Method

◊ Peel and wash the potatoes, season with salt and pepper, cut each into five circles, add rosemary and fry in a frying pan with oil or tail fat until brown.

V Cooled Asparagus
– *Gulanchar Soyutmasy*

Ingredients

◊ 1-2 bunches asparagus

◊ 2 tablespoons apple cider or balsamic vinegar

◊ 2 tablespoons olive oil

Method

◊ Cut off and discard the base of asparagus, then boil the tips for no more than 10 minutes.

◊ Serve, and dress with the vinegar and oil.

◊ Serve either as a hot or cold appetiser.

V Roasted Aubergines and Tomatoes
– Badymjan Pomidor Gizartmasy

Ingredients

◊ 4 aubergines

◊ 6 tomatoes

◊ 6 green sweet peppers

◊ 6 chillis

◊ 4 tablespoons vegetable oil

◊ Salt, to taste

Method

◊ Peel and slice then aubergines into 4 pieces, season each piece with salt and coat with vegetable oil.

◊ Fry in single layers and roast on both sides under the lid. Once cooked, remove from the pan.

◊ Put the whole tomatoes in a frying pan, stew under the lid, fry a little (do not let them fall apart), season with salt. Once cooked, remove from the pan.

◊ Cut the sweet peppers into halves, roast under the lid on both sides and season with salt.

◊ Serve all together with marinade, fresh herbs and soft bread. Best served hot.

V Skewed Kebab Meze
– Kyabab Myazyasi

Ingredients

◊ 6 large aubergines

◊ 6 medium tomatoes

◊ 2 onions

◊ 1 bunch each coriander and basil

◊ Salt, to taste

Method

◊ Slice the aubergines and roast on the grill at a high temperature until browned. Do the same with the tomatoes. Peel and chop the aubergines and tomatoes. Finely chop the onions and herbs and stir thoroughly.

◊ At home, you can brown the aubergines in an old frying pan, bake the tomatoes in the oven, then add the onions and greens straight into the hot mixture of aubergines and tomatoes.

◊ Serve as a snack or side dish to any meat and poultry dish.

Crab Salad a la Baku
– *Baky Salaty*

Ingredients

◊ 250 g crab meat

◊ 300 g pickled red pepper

◊ ½ onion

◊ 100 g sour cream

◊ 1 large bunch coriander

◊ ½ teaspoon chilli powder
(or 3 teaspoons of sweet red pepper)

◊ ½ teaspoon wine or fruit vinegar

Method

◊ Peel and finely chop the crab meat or shrimps. Finely chop the onions, pickled red pepper and coriander, and mix. Dress with the sour cream, pepper and vinegar, and leave in a fridge for 30 minutes.

◊ Serve with coriander. There is no need to add salt.

Soups

> ### Lyatif Abdul Bagi ogly Feizullaev
>
> **Painting:** '*Quiet Shore*' (1968)
>
> Oil on canvas
>
> Signed bottom left corner 'F Latif 68'
>
> 39.4 x 39.4 in (100.0 x 100.0 cm)
>
> **Provenance:** Gift from the painter in 1976.
>
> **Literature:** Bown, M. C., *A Dictionary of Twentieth Century Russian and Soviet Painters 1900 – 1980s*, Izo (1998): 85.
>
> *The Fine Arts of the Azerbaijan SSR*, Sovyetsky Khudozhnik, Moscow (1978): 84 – 85.
>
> The painter Lyatif Abdul Bagi ogly Feizullaev (1918-1980s) was born in Baku. He is an honoured Artist of Azerbaijan SSR. Feizullaev graduated from the Surikov Art Institute in Moscow in 1949. He has participated in numerous exhibitions since 1940. Feizullaev's personal exhibitions in Baku took place in 1961 and 1969, and in Moscow in 1973. His works are presented in Azerbaijan State Museim of Art, Lankaran State Art Gallery, in Vajiha Samadova gallery, in private galleries.

V Sorrel Soup
– *Turshyang*

Ingredients

◊ 1 bunch each sorrel, parsley, celery, dill, coriander, leaves of spring onions

◊ 2 onions

◊ 2 tablespoons melted butter or vegetable oil

◊ 2 boiled eggs

◊ 200 g sour cream

◊ Salt, to taste

Method

◊ Finely chop all the greens. Chop the onions into rings and sauté in butter or oil.

◊ Boil 4 cups of water and drop in all the greens and sautéed onions into it, add salt to taste.

◊ Boil the eggs, cut them into circles, and add to each serving.

◊ Serve with sour cream.

◊ You can cook the same soup using the chicken broth.

V Yoghurt Soup from Gyandzja
– Gyandzja Dovgasy

Ingredients

◊ 4 litres homemade natural yoghurt (gatig)

◊ 50 g rice

◊ 1 egg yolk

◊ 1 heaped tablespoon of flour

◊ 1 bunch each of parsley, mint, dill and coriander (alternatives: parsley, coriander and celery; parsley, coriander and dill; celery, mint and coriander; dill, spinach, celery, coriander or parsley, mint, dill and spinach)

Method

◊ It's better to cook this dish in an aluminum or copper pan, to prevent the bottom from burning.

◊ Stir the natural yoghurt well, boil the rice until tender and add to the yoghurt. Mix the egg yolk with flour and 2 tablespoons of water until smooth, and mix with the yoghurt.

◊ Wash, dry, and finely chop all the greens.

◊ Place the pan over heat and boil the soup stirring it in a steady pace for yoghurt not to clot. When the mixture starts to boil, add the prepared yoghurt, and cook over a low heat for another 5 minutes.

◊ Remove from the heat. Greens have enough natural salt, so season only with pepper to taste.

◊ Serve hot or cold. You can store in the fridge for 5 days and reheat it.

◊ Served cold after a heavy meal to aid digestion.

V Cold Yoghurt-Based Soup with Cucumber and Herbs – *Dograma*

Ingredients

◊ 1 litre homemade yoghurt

◊ 4 fresh cucumbers

◊ 1 bunch each coriander, dill, and basil

◊ ½ onion

◊ Salt, to taste

Method

◊ Add the finely chopped cucumbers, herbs and onion to the natural yoghurt. Season with salt, and add 1 cup of cold water.

◊ Place in the fridge for 30 minutes.

◊ You can add low-fat broth (chicken or beef) instead of water, but it's up to you, since it makes the dish heavier.

◊ Serve in the afternoon and evening, and with bread if desired. This refreshing dish is best served in the heat.

Variation:
V Soup with Spinach – *Ispanach shorbasy*

Ingredients

◊ 2 onions

◊ 1 bunch each of spring onions and spinach

◊ 1 egg

◊ 2 tablespoons any oil or melted butter

◊ 100 g sour cream

◊ 5-10 dried cherry plums or yellow sour plums

Method

◊ Put finely chopped spinach into 1 litre of water.

◊ Finely chop and fry the onion, boil and chop the eggs, drop everything into the broth, add salt and pepper.

◊ Cook for 20 minutes.

◊ Finely chop spring onions and drop into the saucepan before serving.

◊ Serve with sour cream.

◊ This dish can be cooked with the meat or chicken broth.

Offal Dishes

Maral Yusif kizi Rahman-Zade

Painting: *'Fields'* (1964)

Oil on canvas

Inscription on reverse (in Cryllic): '1964/
Fields/Zemiler'

27.6 x 35.4 in (70.0 x 90.0 cm)

Provenance: Acquired by the current owner
in 2011 from a private collection.

Maral Yusif kizi Rahman-Zade (1916 - 2008)
was an Azerbaijani graphic artist, named the
People's Artist of Azerbaijan in 1964, as well
as being a recipient of the State Prize.

Maral Rahman-Zade was born into a family
of goldsmiths in the Absheron village of
Mardakan. In 1940 she graduated from the
Surikov State Art Institute in Moscow, after
which she returned to Baku.

Sheep Testis
– *Khaya Gyzartmasi*

Ingredients

◊ 500 g sheep or cow testis

◊ 200 g fruit vinegar or sherry

◊ 1 pomegranate

Method

◊ Cut the testis into small pieces, soak in balsamic vinegar or sherry. Leave to soak for 1 hour.

◊ Drain the liquid, heat the oil and fry for 5 minutes. This is one of the rare delicacies. Add salt to taste.

◊ To serve, sprinkle with pomegranate seeds.

Main Dishes - Meat

Stewed Meat, Aubergines, Tomatoes and Peppers – *Ajapsandal*

Ingredients

◊ 500 g lamb

◊ 6 aubergines

◊ 6 tomatoes

◊ 5 green sweet peppers (recommended thin-skinned)

◊ 3 onions

◊ 1 tablespoon oil

◊ 1 teaspoon turmeric

◊ Salt and pepper, to taste

Method

◊ Chop the meat and onions and sauté them together.

◊ Peel the aubergines, slice them in circles (as think as your finger) and place in a layer covering the meat.

◊ Peel and half the tomatoes (easier if scalded).

◊ Place a layer of sweet peppers cut into rings over the aubergines and cover them with a layer of tomatoes. Add salt and pepper, ½ cup of water and stew at a low temperature until the meat is cooked (40 minutes), sprinkle with turmeric and leave for 10-15 minutes.

◊ Serve with fresh green salads and pickles.

Aubergine, Tomatoes and Green Peppers Stuffed with Meat
– *Badymjan, Pomidor, Bibar Dolmasy*

Ingredients

◊ 1 kg lamb, beef or veal

◊ 3 onion heads

◊ 8 of each – medium aubergines, tomatoes, and sweet thin-skinned peppers

◊ 2 bunches rayhan (purple or green basil)

◊ 1 tablespoon turmeric

◊ 500 g yoghurt

◊ 2-3 cloves garlic (for the garlic-yoghurt sauce)

◊ Salt, black pepper – optional

Method

◊ Crop the stalks of the aubergines, make short longitudinal cuts, blanche them in boiling water and let them cool down.

◊ Cut the top of tomatoes and remove ⅓ of the pulp. Cut the top off of the peppers and de-seed. Keep the tops of the tomatoes and peppers for later.

◊ Mix the salt and turmeric on a plate.

◊ Grind the meat in the meat grinder and fry it with the chopped onion (do not dry it, the mince meat should remain juicy).

◊ Add the chopped basil and tomato pulp into the mince meat and mix thoroughly, adding salt and pepper.

◊ Coat the inside of the aubergines, tomatoes and peppers with the salt and turmeric mixture and fill them with the mince meat. Cover the tomatoes and peppers with their cut off tops. Place them in a wide and deep pan in layers: aubergines on the bottom, then tomatoes and pepper.

◊ Pour ½ glass of water, cover with a lid and stew until the water completely boils out. Place one aubergine, one tomato and one pepper on a plate. On top pour the garlic-yoghurt sauce or pure natural organic yoghurt. Stuffed aubergines, stuffed tomatoes and stuffed peppers may be prepared separately with the same stuffing.

◊ Each of these dishes can be served independently. However, when they are prepared all together, a different aroma and taste is achieved.

◊ Please see the following page for a variation on this classic dish.

Variation:
V Aubergine Stuffed with Vegetables
– *Terevez Badymjan Dolmasy*

Ingredients

◊ 6 aubergines

◊ 2 carrots

◊ 2 sweet peppers

◊ 1 bunch each parsley, celery

◊ 1 bunch basil (can be dried)

◊ 2 tablespoons vegetable oil

◊ 1 onion

◊ Salt, 2 teaspoons of turmeric and pepper to taste

Method

◊ Remove the aubergine's fruit stalk, make a small axial cut, parboil in boiling water, remove, put under the press and cool.

◊ Finely chop the carrots, peppers, onion and sauté. Finely chop the basil and combine all the ingredients.

◊ Coat each aubergine with a mixture of salt, pepper and turmeric on the inside and put into a roasting pan or a deep frying pan, add oil, ½ glass of water and stew until the water reduces so that only oil remains.

◊ Serve as a hot second course or as a cold snack.

◊ * If you want to prevent the bottom of the pan from burning, layer it with some meat bones.

Shepherd's Stewed Meat
– *Kyalapyr*

Ingredients

◊ 2-3 kg of lamb, veal or beef (ribs, shank, brisket meat)

◊ Natural yoghurt with garlic or plain natural yoghurt

◊ 1 bunch of dill

◊ 2-3 cloves of garlic

◊ Thyme and rosemary

◊ Salt and pepper, to taste

Method

◊ Cut the meat and put in a large wok or aluminium saucepan, season with salt and pepper, add 500 g of water and boil at a low temperature until the meat is cooked (add water, if necessary). There should be a thick broth in the bottom.

◊ Serve hot, pouring the broth on the meat. Garnish with garlic yoghurt or plain yoghurt and fresh finely chopped dill.

◊ Serve with fresh onions or spring onions, fresh greens, tomatoes and bread.

◊ Season with 2 teaspoons of thyme and rosemary.

Mince Meat Sausages with Onion and Eggs – *Shamkyabab*

Ingredients

◊ 800 g boneless lamb, veal or beef

◊ 4 onions - 2 diced, 2 sliced

◊ 4 eggs

◊ Juice 2 lemons

◊ 1 pinch turmeric

◊ 4 tablespoons olive oil or melted butter

◊ Salt and pepper, to taste

Method

◊ Prepare a mixture of meat and 2 onions, add turmeric, salt, and stir thoroughly.

◊ Form small sausages from the mixture (5-6 cm in size) and sauté them on both sides.

◊ Sauté the sliced onions in oil or butter.

◊ Cook an omelette from the beaten eggs and slice into portions.

◊ Place the sautéed meat sausages, onions and eggs in a deep frying pan, add lemon juice or citric acid, or a paste of cherry plums, add ½ glass of water and stew for 30 minutes at a low temperature.

◊ Serve with fresh green salad or some marinades.

Main Dishes - Poultry

Chicken Stew with Omelette
– *Toyug Chygyrtmasy*

Ingredients

◊ 1 whole chicken

◊ 2 onion heads

◊ ½ teaspoon citric acid or juice of 1 lemon

◊ 2 eggs

◊ 2 tablespoons vegetable oil or clarified butter

◊ Salt, pepper – optional

Method

◊ Boil the chicken (the broth may be used for a soup), cool down, add salt, pepper, cut into pieces.

◊ Sauté the onion rings.

◊ Prepare omelette with two eggs.

◊ Lay the cooked chicken on a pan, pour it over the marinated onion, sprinkle with citric acid or lemon juice.

◊ Serve the omelette on top in portions.

◊ Pour over ½ cup of the broth and stew for 20 minutes.

◊ Serve the dish with the omelette on top.

Chicken and Vegetable Stew
– *Toyug Terevez Buglamasy*

Ingredients

◊ 1 whole chicken

◊ 1 onion head

◊ 3 sweet bell peppers

◊ 6 medium tomatoes

◊ 2 tablespoons oil

◊ Salt – optional

Method

◊ Cut the chicken into 6 pieces, stew with chopped onions, then lightly sauté.

◊ Separately steam the whole tomatoes until soft, cut each pepper in half longitudinally and fry under a lid for 5 minutes.

◊ Put the chicken, tomatoes and pepper in a deep pan but do not mix them, stew all together for 20 minutes.

◊ Serve on a large dish. Chicken in the middle, peppers and tomatoes on the side.

Roast Guinea Fowl
– *Shakhgushu Sobada*

Ingredients

◊ 1 whole guinea fowl

◊ 3 sour green apples

◊ 2 oranges

◊ Salt, pepper – optional

Method

◊ Wash the guinea fowl, add salt on the inside and outside. Cut the apples into 6-8 slices, remove the centre.

◊ Cut the oranges into disks. Stuff the hen with apples and oranges.

◊ Put the guinea fowl in foil, surround it with the remaining fruits and wrap tightly.

◊ Pour 3 cups of water on a tray and place the foil parcel onto the tray.

◊ Bake for 4 hours at 200°C.

◊ Unwrap the cooked guinea fowl, and serve with the remaining juice.

Main Dishes - Fish

Lyatif Abdul Bagi ogly Feizullaev

Painting: 'Calm Shore' (1974)

Oil on canvas

Signed bottom left corner 'F Latif 74'

21.9 x 23.6 in (55.7 x 60.0 cm)

Provenance: Acquired by the current owner in 2000.

Literature: Bown, M. C., *A Dictionary of Twentieth Century Russian and Soviet Painters 1900 – 1980s*, Izo (1998): 85.

The Fine Arts of the Azerbaijan SSR, Sovyetsky Khudozhnik, Moscow (1978): 84 – 85.

The painter Lyatif Abdul Bagi ogly Feizullaev (1918-1980s) was born in Baku. He is an honoured Artist of Azerbaijan SSR. Feizullaev graduated from the Surikov Art Institute in Moscow in 1949. He has participated in numerous exhibitions since 1940. Feizullaev's personal exhibitions in Baku took place in 1961 and 1969, and in Moscow in 1973. His works are presented in Azerbaijan State Museim of Art, Lankaran State Art Gallery, in Vajiha Samadova gallery, in private galleries.

Sautéed Lamprey with Sumac
– *Ilanbalygy Gyzartmasy*

Ingredients

◊ 2-3 lampreys

◊ 1 pomegranate

◊ 2 tablespoons sumac

◊ 4 tablespoons vegetable oil

◊ 3 tablespoons flour

◊ Salt, pepper – optional

Method

◊ Wash and dry the fish and cut it into 2 or 3 parts (approximately 10 cm in size). Season with salt and pepper.

◊ Roll in the flour and fry on both sides in a very hot pan under a lid, for no longer than 10 minutes.

◊ Serve, and sprinkle with sumac and pomegranate seeds.

Salmon and Vegetables Stew
– *Gyzylbalyg Buglamasy*

Ingredients

◊ 1 kg salmon

◊ 2 aubergines

◊ 4 tomatoes

◊ 3 bell peppers

◊ 3 onion

◊ ½ teaspoon turmeric

◊ 3 tablespoons vegetable oil

◊ Salt, pepper – optional

Method

◊ Cut the fish into steaks 2 cm thick.

◊ Cut the aubergines, peppers and onions into rings, and the tomatoes into halves.

◊ Put the onions on the bottom of a stew pot or a deep pan, then add aubergines, fish, peppers and tomatoes. Add salt, pepper and sprinkle with turmeric on the top.

◊ Stew for 30 minutes on a medium heat until ready, and then reduce to a low heat.

Main Dishes - Pilaffs

Draught Cornus Fruit or Sour Cherry Pilaff – *Zogalli Ash*

Ingredients

◊ 500 g lamb

◊ 2 onions

◊ 2 cups rice

◊ 250 g dried or fresh cornus fruits – pitted, fresh or frozen sour cherries (we have different kinds in the shops for example Early Richmond cherries, Morello or Montmerency)

◊ 50 g tail fat or 1 tablespoons olive oil/clarified butter)

◊ 50 g butter

◊ Salt – optional

Method

◊ Chop the meat (1.5 x 1.5 cm) and onions, fry them to brownish crust (add the olive oil or clarified butter or tail fat if the meat is not too greasy), pour 1 cup of water and stew until the meat is ready.

◊ Rinse the previously soaked rice and pour it into a pot with the meat, put the cornus fruit on top, add salt and pour in cold water so that the water covers the rice by two finger's thickness.

◊ Wrap the lid in towel, cover the pan tightly and cook on low heat using an absorbtion method for 30-40 mins until the rice is ready.

◊ The water should evaporate completely. Add the butter on top of the rice and leave off the heat with the the lid on for 5-10 minutes.

◊ Serve with greenery, marinades and fresh vegetables.

Kebabs

Samed Yunus ogly Akhverdov

Painting: *'Illuminated Mountains'* (undated)

Oil on canvas

Not signed

27.6 x 35.4 in (108.3 x 108.0 cm)

Provenance: Acquired by the current owner in 1981.

Literature: Bown, M. C., *A Dictionary of Twentieth Century Russian and Soviet Painters 1900 – 1980s*, Izo (1998): 7.

The Fine Arts of the Azerbaijan SSR, Sovyetsky Khudozhnik, Moscow (1978): 17.

The painter Samed Yunus ogly Akhverdov was born in 1921 in Baku, Azerbaijan. In 1944 he graduated from the State Art Academy of Azerbaijan named after A. Azimzade.

Akhverdov has participated in numerous art exhibitions since 1946. He had a personal exhibition in Baku which took place in 1971. Akhverdov was a Member of the USSR Guild of Artists. He died in 1991

Marinated Baby Lamb Kebab
– *Bastyrma Kyabab*

Ingredients

◊ 3-4 kg baby lamb

◊ 1 kg onion

◊ Salt, pepper – optional

Method

◊ Cut the meat into slices (4 x 4 cm), chop the onion and mix it with the meat, add salt, pepper, lay the meat in an enamelled pot and leave in a cold place for a day.

◊ When cooking, shake the onions off, string the meat on skewers and place on the brazier. Turn the skewers 2-3 times. The meat is very tender and cooks very fast. Do not burn! Serve with sumac, fresh greens, salads with greens and tomatoes, fresh chopped onions. Generally, it is good to place slices of sheep tail fat (4 x 4 cm) when slicing the meat for shashlik and preparing basturma. The slices of tail fat should be strung on the skewers separately as the cooking time varies. The tail fat should be brown like fried potatoes. Serve with other kinds of vegetable kebab.

Lulah Kebab

Ingredients

◊ 1.5 kg lamb meat

◊ 100 g tail fat

◊ 3 onion heads

◊ 100 g sumac

◊ Salt, pepper – optional

Method

◊ Pass the lamb meat and onions through a meat grinder twice, add salt and pepper, and leave for 30 min.

◊ Form short sausages, string them on skewers and place on the prepared brazier. Cook for 10-15 minutes.

◊ Serve with lavash, churek, phyllo, fresh herbs and onions. Sprinkle with sumac.

◊ Lulah kebab may be prepared from veal or turkey if 300 g of tail fat is added for 1.5 kg of meat. Method of preparation is the same.

V Aubergine Kebab

Ingredients

◊ 8-10 medium aubergines

◊ 2 onion heads

◊ Basil, coriander – optional

Method

◊ Wash the aubergines and string 3-4 of each transversely on skewers, place them on well heated brazier. The skin should become scarred and cracked.

◊ Serve the kebabs, sprinkle with the fresh herbs and chopped onions.

◊ Serve as a side dish with meat kebabs.

V Potato Lulah Kebab

Ingredients

◊ 1 kg potatoes
◊ 200 g tail fat
◊ Salt, pepper – optional

Method

◊ Peel and boil the potatoes, mash them into a purée, add ground tail fat, mix thoroughly and pass through a meat grinder once more. Add salt and pepper. Form little sausages on the skewers and place them on a prepared brazier. Fry on both sides for 3-5 minutes. Serve with any meat kebab.
◊ See below for variations.

V Potatoes in Ashes

Method

◊ Wash the potatoes and bury them in the ashes remaining in the brazier after preparation of shashlik. The potatoes will be ready in an hour.
◊ Serve with any meat kebab.

V Tomato Kebab

Ingredients

◊ Medium sized tomatoes – as required per serving.

Method

◊ Wash the tomatoes thoroughly, dry them and thread on to the skewers. Fry on both sides for 15-20 minutes.
◊ Serve with any meat kebab.

V Green Pepper Kebab

Method

◊ Thread long green peppers on skewers, fry and serve with shashlik.
◊ Serve with any meat kebab.

V Kebab Mezesi

Method

◊ Bake the tomatoes and aubergines on the brazier, clean, mash, stuff with raw onion, rayhan (basil) and coriander. Mix thoroughly. Serve with any meat kebab.

Dough Dishes

Emin Mamedov

Painting: *'Sunset'* (undated)
Oil on canvas
Inscription on reverse (in Cyrillic): 'Sunset
65,5 x 50.'
19.7 x 25.6 in (50 x 65 cm)
Provenance: Presented by artist the current
owner in 2008.

Emin Mamedov was born in 1968. Emin
studied at the Surikov Institute in Moscow.
Now, Emin works and lives in Baku.

V Diamond-Shaped Pasta with Sautéed Onions, Tomatoes and Eggs
– *Soganchaly Siuzmya Hangyal*

Ingredients

◊ 1 kg flour

◊ 3 eggs

◊ 3 onion heads

◊ 3 tomatoes (or 1 tablespoon of tomato paste)

◊ 3 tablespoons oil

◊ Garlic

◊ Yoghurt sauce (sarmisagli gatig)

◊ Salt – optional

Method

◊ Prepare stiff dough with flour, egg, a pinch of salt and 2-2½ cups of water.

◊ Knead the dough, divide into balls the size of a tennis ball and roll each ball to a thin state. Then cut the dough into diamonds 5-6 cm in size and pat them dry.

◊ Sauté the onion rings in oil, make an omelette with the 2 eggs and cut into portions. Slice and steam the tomatoes, then combine all the ingredients (if there are no tomatoes available, tomato paste may be used).

◊ Boil the diamond shaped dough in a salty water then strain, and serve with the garlic-gatig sauce, sautéed onions, tomatoes and omelette.

Desserts, Jams and Beverages

Sattar Bakhul ogly Bakhlul-Zade

Painting: *'Fig Trees by the Sea'* (1967)

Oil on composite board

Signed bottom right (in Azeri): 'hermetil Magsuda/ khatira Satta an...'; inscription on reverse (in Cryllic): 'Dear Tofik Useynov/ Wishing you happiness/9.6.82 Maksud'

33.3 x 36.0 in (84.5 x 91.5 cm)

Provenance: Acquired by the current owner in 1982.

Literature: Bown, M. C., *A Dictionary of Twentieth Century Russian and Soviet Painters 1900 – 1980s*, Izo (1998):22.

The Fine Arts of the Azerbaijan SSR, Sovyetsky Khudozhnik, Moscow (1978): 22 – 25.

Sattar Bakhlul ogly Bakhlul-Zade (1909-1974) was born in Amiradjan, a village near Baku. He was named the People's Artist of Azerbaijan SSR, and granted the National Azerbaijan SSR award. His artistic education began in 1933 in the Drawing Department at the Moscow Surikov Fine Arts Institute, where he studied under Vladimir Favorsky. During summer workshops in the Crimea, the Russian painter Marc Chagall saw some of Bakhlul-Zade's sketches and suggested that he transfer to the Institute's Painting Department.

Bakhlul-Zade began exhibiting in 1940. His solo exhibitions include: Baku (1955, 1960, 1974), Yerevan (1956), Tbilisi (1956), Moscow (1965, 1973), and the National Gallery in Prague (1964/6). After the exhibition in Prague five of his works were selected for the museum's collection.

V Watermelon Rind Jam
– *Garpyz Miuryabbyasi*

Ingredients

◊ 1 kg clean watermelon rind

◊ 1½ kg granulated sugar

◊ 10 carnations

◊ 2 tablespoons baking soda

◊ 1 litre water

Method

◊ Remove the green layer on the bottom and pink layer on the top of a watermelon with thick rinds.

◊ Cut into shapes, cover with water and add baking soda. Leave for 5-6 hours.

◊ Then wash under flowing water, boil once in clean water and drain.

◊ Prepare a syrup, dip the rinds into it and boil for 20 minutes. Then leave it for 12 hours and then boil again for 20 minutes and add carnations.

◊ Put into jars.

V Fig Jam – *Injil Miuryabbyasi*

Ingredients

◊ 1 kg yellow figs

◊ 1 kg granulated sugar

◊ 10 carnations

◊ 1 cup water

Method

◊ Wash the figs, make holes in them and put in boiling syrup – leave overnight.

◊ Boil on a high heat, removing the foam, until it is ready.

◊ Put in jars and add the carnations.

V   Refreshing Drink
– *Khosȟab*

Ingredients

◊   200 g each – dried fruits: dried apricots, cherry-plum, plum, prune

◊   2 litres water

◊   Salt – optional

Method

◊   Wash the dry fruits thoroughly and pour boiling water over them. Do not boil, put aside for a day at room temperature.

◊   Mix thoroughly and put into the fridge. The beverage is pleasant to taste, and has the natural sweetness of dried fruits.

V   Extract from Mulberry with Fruits Inside – *Irchal*

Ingredients

◊   3-4 kg mulberry

◊   ½ cup water

Method

◊   Cook in the same way as bekmez but with the fruits until it thickens.

◊   Put into jars.

Cultured Milk Dishes

V Organic Homemade Natural Yoghurt – *Katyk*

Ingredients

◊ 2 litres milk (whole milk of 3.5% or more milkfat)

◊ 2 teaspoons sour dough

Method

◊ Warm the milk to 40°C and pour into the glass jars. Put the jars on a linen towel and check the temperature with your finger. The milk should slightly burn a finger.

◊ Add a teaspoon of the sour dough (make sour dough for the first time from yoghurt and sour cream, and later on leave some yoghurt to prepare sour dough) in each jar.

◊ Cover the jars with the lids, wrap with some woollen cloth and leave. Open in 5 hours and cool to the room temperature. Put in the fridge, so that the mass becomes solid.

◊ This recipe is great for babies/toddlers from 5 months old. This recipe is for a cold side dish at breakfast or as a snack.

V Refreshing Drink Made of Natural Yoghurt – *Ayran*

Ingredients

◊ 500 g natural yoghurt

◊ ½ bunch dill

◊ 200 g water

◊ Salt, to taste

Method

◊ Dissolve the natural yoghurt with water, finely chop the dill and add salt, to taste.

◊ Cool well and serve with any dish and as a cold refreshing drink.

V Strained Yoghurt
– *Siuzmya Katyk*

Ingredients

◊ 5-6 litres natural yoghurt

◊ Salt, to taste

Method

◊ Pour the natural yoghurt into a linen bag and hang.

◊ The sour dough will drip gradually, and you will get a mass similar to dietetic cottage cheese. You can put it in a glass or enamelled ware or leave in a bag, add salt and serve for breakfast.

◊ It stores well and for a long period of time.

◊ Siuzmya can be used for making sandwiches by spreading on the bread or crackers for breakfast.

◊ This recipe is great for babies of over 6 months.

Variation 1:
V Strained Yoghurt with Cucumber
– *Hiyarly Siuzmya*

Ingredients

◊ 300 g siuzmya

◊ 3 fresh cucumbers

◊ Salt, to taste

Method

◊ Finely chop the cucumbers and mix together with the siuzmya. Add salt.

◊ Serve as a snack with sandwiches, or as a spread for pita bread (lavash), bread or croutons.

Variation 2:
V Strained Yoghurt with Herbs
– *Keshnishli Siuzmya*

Ingredients

◊ 300 g siuzmya

◊ Dill and tarragon or basil or coriander

◊ Salt, to taste

Method

◊ Mix the siuzmya with the finely chopped herbs, and add salt to taste.

◊ Serve with flatbread like churek or pita bread (lavash) or any other bread.

V Rolls Made of Thin Lavash Stuffed with Sheep's Milk Cheese or Feta and Herbs – *Dyurtmya*

Ingredients

◊ Thin tortilla or lavash

◊ 20 g sheep's milk cheese or feta

◊ A leaf spring onions

◊ 1 bunch each coriander, tarragon, basil and mint

Method

◊ This dish is cooked in portions.

◊ Crush the cheese (sheep's milk cheese) or feta on a half of a tortilla or lavash, sprinkle with the chopped spring onions, tarragon and basil or coriander and make a roll (roll it so that it had only one hole on one of the sides).

◊ Can be served as a snack before dinner or with sweet tea. The tortilla can be served cold or warmed in the oven.

V Melon and Cheese Snack
Yemish-Pendir Myazyasi

Ingredients

◊ Melon

◊ Sheep's milk cheese or feta

◊ Tortilla or lavash

◊ Dry red wine, to taste

Method

◊ Slice the melon.

◊ Envelope the cheese in a thin tortilla or lavash.

◊ Serve as a snack.

◊ Melon and cheese (any white cheese) can be served without tortilla or lavash, with red dry wine.

V Grapes and Cheese
– *Izium-Pendir Myazyasi*

Ingredients

◊ A selection of grapes

◊ Sheep's milk cheese, feta or other white cheese

◊ Thin tortilla, pita bread or lavash – optional

Method

◊ Envelope the cheese in a thin tortilla, pita bread or lavash.

◊ Serve with the grapes and red wine.

V Watermelon and Cheese
– *Garpyz-Pendir Myazyasi*

Ingredients

◊ Watermelon

◊ Sheep's milk cheese or feta

◊ Thin tortilla or lavash

Method

◊ Envelope the cheese in a lavash and eat with the watermelon.

◊ Can be served without lavash with some good red wine.

Autumn

Starters – Salads and Hot and Cold Appetisers

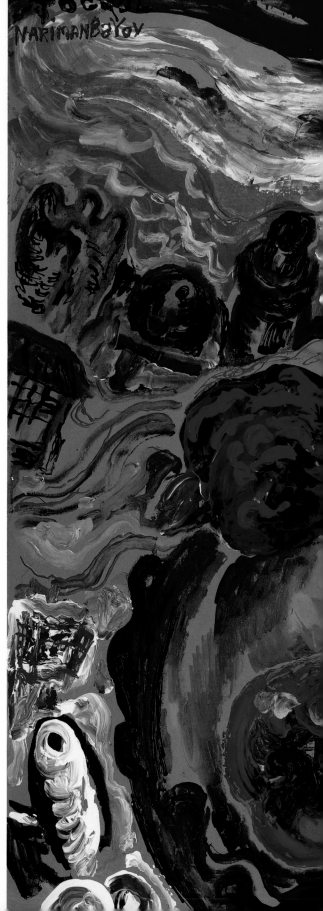

Togrul Farman ogly Narimanbekov

Painting: *'In ancient Baku'* (undated)

Oil on canvas

Signed top left: 'Togrul Narimanbayov'; inscription on reverse (central section in Cyrillic): 'Togrul Narimanbayov/In Ancient Baku/Narimanbekov Togrul'

35.4 x 39.3 in (90.0 x 99.7 cm)

Provenance: Acquired by the current owner in 2010.

Literature: Bown, M. C., *A Dictionary of Twentieth Century Russian and Soviet Painters 1900 – 1980s*, Izo (1998): 218.

The Fine Arts of the Azerbaijan SSR, Sovyetsky Khudozhnik, Moscow (1978): 59 - 62.

Togrul Farman ogly Narimanbekov was born in Baku in 1930. He is the honoured artist of the Azerbaijan SSR, laureate of the Azerbaijan State Prize and laureate of the Azerbaijan Lenin Comsomol prize. Narimanbekov studied at the Baku Art College until 1950. In 1955 he graduated from the Vilnyus Art Institute. Narimanbekov began exhibiting around 1952. His personal exhibitions include: Baku, 1961, 1965, 1975; Moscow, 1967, 1972; Vilnyus, 1972; Volgograd, 1973; Prague, 1965; Wroclaw, Warsaw, Sopot, 1973; and Lviv, 1975. Narimanbekov was also vice-president of the Committee for Solidarity of Asia and Africa (1973) and a member of the Peace Committee (1981). He died in Paris in 2013.

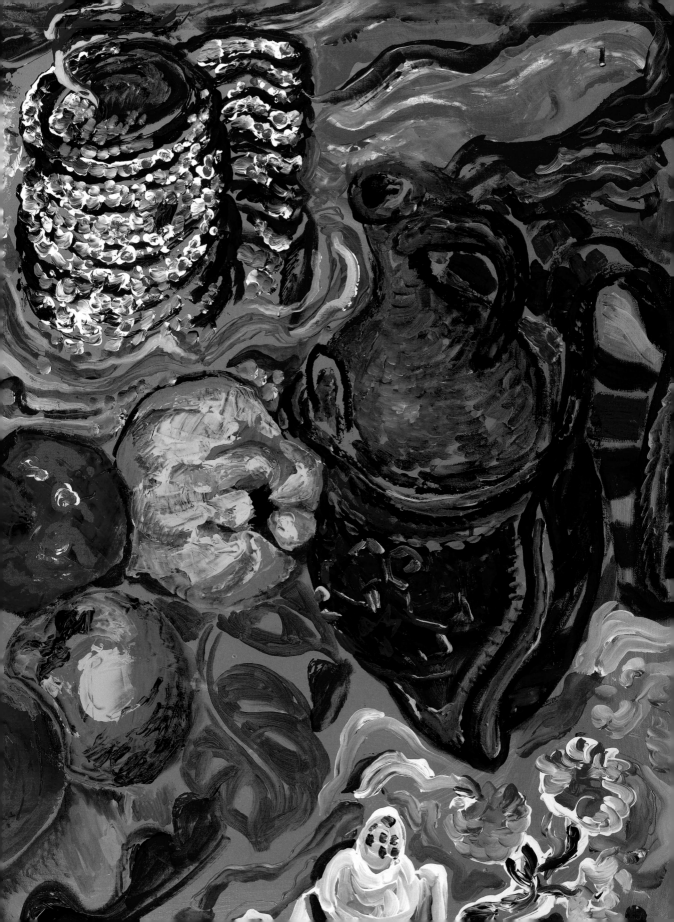

V Sautéed Aubergines
– *Badymjan Sautesi*

Ingredients

◊ 3 aubergines

◊ 3 sweet green peppers

◊ 1 hot pepper (to taste, for piquancy)

◊ Vegetable oil

Method

◊ Wash the aubergines without peeling off the skins, and cut into rings. Add salt to taste. Put into the frying pan, add ¼ cup of water and cover. Stew for 10 minutes to allow the aubergines to soften. Cut the sweet pepper into slices, split the chilli in half and add all to the aubergines. Add the olive oil, and cover the frying pan with the lid. Cook for 15-20 minutes to fry the aubergines, stirring occasionally. Serve hot with tomato salad or with meat or fish. When cold, spread on toasted bread.

◊ This recipe can be served as a hot or cold starter, or as a side dish.

V Fennel Salad
– Changyt Salaty

Ingredients

◊ 2 fennel bulbs

◊ 1 red sweet pepper

◊ 1 large lemon

◊ 3 tablespoons olive oil

◊ 1 bunch of coriander

◊ Pomegranate seeds

◊ Diced cucumber

◊ Baby potatoes and baby broccoli – optional

◊ Salt and pepper, to taste

Method

◊ Cut the fennel into circles, the sweet pepper and cucumbers into small squares, and chop the coriander. Add the olive oil, squeeze in the lemon and add the pomegranate. Toss all of the ingredients together. Serve as a side dish with fish, poultry or meat.

◊ This recipe can be served as a starter or as a side dish to a main course.

V Salad with Onion, Herbs and Vinegar – *Sogan-Gey Salaty*

Ingredients

◊ 1 onion

◊ ½ bunch of coriander and dill each

◊ 2 tablespoons each of vinegar and olive oil

◊ Salt and pepper, to taste

Method

◊ Cut the onion into rings.

◊ Finely chop the herbs, season with salt, and mix with the onion.

◊ Dress with a mixture of vinegar and olive oil.

V Autumn Salad
– *Payiz Salaty*

Ingredients

◊ 2 tomatoes

◊ 1 cucumber

◊ ½ bunch each of coriander or mint

◊ Salt, to taste

Method

◊ Dice tomatoes and a cucumber. Season lightly with salt, sprinkle with coriander or mint and mix the ingredients.

◊ Serve without dressing, since the vegetables have their own juices.

V Salad with Pomegranate – *Nar Salaty*

Ingredients

◊ 2-3 pomegranates

◊ 1 onion

◊ 1 bunch of corianderand dill

◊ Green peppers

◊ Salt, to taste

Method

◊ De-seed the pomegranates and squeeze the juice out of them. Finely chop the coriander, green peppers, onions, and dill, and mix together with the pomegranate juice and seeds. Season with salt.

◊ This salad could be served as garnish for any meat, fish, poultry and vegetable dish, or any pilaff.

V Cauliflower Salad
– *Gül Kelem Soyutmasy*

Ingredients

◊ 1 cauliflower head

◊ 500 g organic natural yoghurt

◊ Pitta bread or thin lavash

◊ Salt, to taste

Method

◊ Wash and steam-cook the cauliflower in salted water. Let cool and cut into florets.

◊ Separately serve some yoghurt, and sprinkle dried or fresh mint. It can be also served with sheep's milk cheese, pitta bread or lavash.

◊ This dish should be served cold.

V Fried Pumpkin Stew
– *Balgabag Govurmasy*

Ingredients

◊ 1 kg pumpkin

◊ 3-4 tablespoons vegetable oil

◊ 2 onions

◊ Salt, to taste

Method

◊ Wash, dice and sauté the pumpkin in oil under the lid.

◊ Chop and sauté the onions.

◊ Mix the onions with the pumpkin, add salt and stew together for approximately 10 minutes.

◊ This can also be used as a side dish to any meat, fish or poultry dishes.

Soups

Usein Izzet ogly Kerimov

Painting: '*Fishermen*' (undated)

Oil on canvas

Signed on reverse (in Cyrillic): 'Kerimov'

28.0 x 44.1 in (71.0 x 112.0 cm)

Provenance: Acquired by the current owner in 2010.

Literature: Bown, M. C., *A Dictionary of Twentieth Century Russian and Soviet Painters 1900 – 1980s*, Izo (1998): 131.

The Fine Arts of the Azerbaijan SSR, Sovyetsky Khudozhnik, Moscow (1978): 45.

Usein Izzet ogly Kerimov was born in Baku, Azerbaijan, in 1925. He graduated from the Baku Art College in 1945 and from the Moscow Surikov Art Institute in 1952. Kerimov began exhibiting in 1947 and between 1979 and 1982 he taught at the Baku Polytechnic Institute. Kerimov died in 1992.

Fish Soup
– *Balyg Shorbasy*

Ingredients

◊ 1 kg sturgeon (European sturgeon or swordfish if you can't find sturgeon)

◊ 5 onions

◊ 6-7 bay leaves

◊ 10-15 allspices (whole)

◊ 200 g tomato paste

◊ ¼ teaspoon chilli pepper or 3 tablespoons sweet pepper

◊ 1 egg yolk

◊ 1 flat tablespoon flour

◊ 2 large bunches parsley

◊ Salt, to taste

Method

◊ Chop all the onions very finely and drop them in 3 litres of water, then add the bay leaves, allspices, finely chopped parsley, season with salt, and cook for 30 minutes over a low heat (onions should get perfectly tender).

◊ Cut sturgeon into large pieces and drop in the soup together with the chilli pepper and tomato paste. Cook for 30 minutes.

◊ Mix the yolks with the flour and ¼ cup of water and pour them into the boiling soup stirring it at a steady pace. Turn off the heat and let the soup draw. The more infused this soup, the tastier it is.

◊ Make a mash out of 3 tablespoons of tomato paste and 1 tablespoon of powdered chilli pepper and serve it separately for those who like spicy dishes.

V Soup with Beans
– *Lobiya Shorbasy*

Ingredients

◊ 200 g red or spotted beans

◊ 2 onions

◊ 10-15 dried cherry plums, dried sour yellow plums, or prunes

◊ 2 bunches parsley

◊ 1 bunch coriander

◊ 2 tablespoons vegetable oil

◊ 1 tablespoon tomato paste

◊ 1 tablespoon vinegar

◊ 1 quince

◊ Salt and pepper, to taste

Method

◊ Cover the beans with boiling water overnight, so that the water covers the beans by up to 2 cm.

◊ When the beans swell, add 500 g of water, 1 onion, sliced quince, cherry plums and dried sour yellow plums (or prunes), and cook until beans become tender.

◊ Finely chop the remaining onion and sauté it.

◊ Add finely chopped parsley, the sautéed onions, tomato paste and vinegar to the cooked beans, season with pepper and salt. Cook for 35 minutes.

◊ The soup should be thick.

◊ Drop finely chopped coriander in a pan before serving.

Offal Dishes

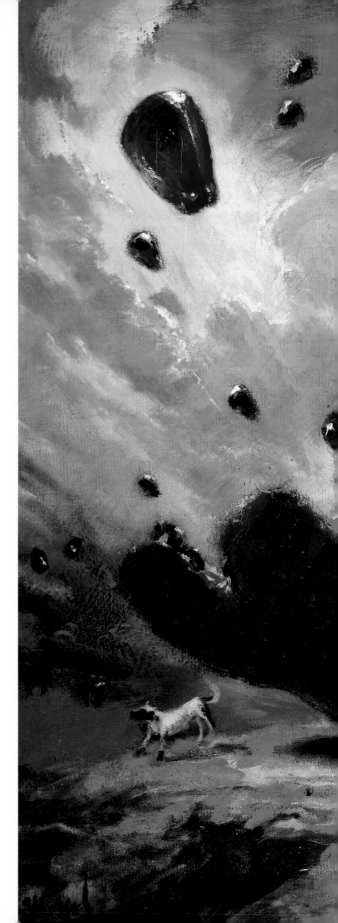

Oleg Ibrahim ogly Ibrahimov

Painting: *Giant Pomegranate* (undated)

Oil on canvas

Signed bottom left left (in Cyrillic): 'Ibragimaov'

30.4 x 34.4 in (80.7 x 100.7 cm)

Provenance: Presented by the artist for the current owner in 1981.

Literature: Bown, M. C., *A Dictionary of Twentieth Century Russian and Soviet Painters 1900 – 1980s*, Izo (1998): 113.

Oleg Ibrahim ogly Ibrahimov was born in Baku in 1943 to the family of the poet Ibrahim Kabirli. After completing high school, the gifted young man studied at the Moscow Surikov Institute and the Mukhina Leningrad Higher School of Industrial Art.

In 1976, as part of the Central Committee of the Communist Youth League at the height of the Brezhnev era, the young artist was sent to the Baikal-Amur Mainline, whose grand-scale construction project later inspired a lot of his work. Back in Moscow, Ibrahimov opened his solo exhibition at the "Manezh" exhibition space, which caused great enthusiasm amongst the Soviet press. Ibrahimov is also a member of the USSR Guild of Artists.

In 2008 Ibrahimov had his solo show in the "Yaradan" exhibition hall in Baku. His paintings have also been exhibited in Moscow and St.Petersburg in the framework of the Decade of Azerbaijani Culture in the Russian Federation, as well as in the best salons in Finland, Morocco, Bulgaria, Poland, Germany, the Czech Republic and other countries.

Sheep Brain Stew
– *Beyin Buglamasy*

Ingredients

◊ 500 g sheep brain

◊ 2 onions

◊ 2 tablespoons clarified butter

◊ Pomegranate seeds

◊ Salt, pepper, sumac – to taste

Method

◊ Boil the sheep brains and cut it into pieces. Sauté the onion in oil and mix with the brain.

◊ Stew them together for 10-15 minutes, add salt, pepper, sprinkle with sumac or pomegranate seeds.

◊ Serve as hot appetiser.

Chicken Offal Stew
– *Toyug Ichalaty Buglamasy*

Ingredients

◊   1 kg chicken offal (preferably heart and liver)

◊   2 onion heads

◊   3 tablespoons vegetable oil

◊   Pomegranate seeds

◊   Salt – optional

Method

◊   Stew the chicken offal in a pan for 10-15 minutes with ½ cup of water. Sauté the onion rings in oil and mix them with the offal. Add salt to taste.

◊   Serve with chopped onions and vinegar-garlic sauce.

◊   Sprinkle with pomegranate seeds.

◊   For a variation of this dish, see below.

Variation: Kidneys Stew
– *Beirek Buglamasy*

Ingredients

◊   500 g veal or lamb kidneys

◊   2 onions

◊   2 tablespoons of plum extract

◊   3 tablespoons vegetable oil

◊   Salt, pepper – to taste

Method

◊   Cut the kidneys into 4 parts, wash thoroughly and let them sit in water for 1 hour. Drain the water and steam until ready. Add plum and sour lavash or lemon juice.

◊   Sauté the onion rings in oil and mix with the kidneys, adding salt and pepper to taste. Steam them together for 10 minutes.

◊   Serve hot with marinades and salads.

Main Dishes - Meat

Tagi Aziz Aga ogly Tagiev

Painting: '*Bus in the Mountains*' (1965)

Oil on canvas

Inscription on the reverse (in Cyrillic):
'Tagiev Tagi 1965'.

27.8 x 53.7 in (70.7 x 136.5 cm)

Provenance: Acquired by the current owner in 2010.

Literature: Bown, M. C., *A Dictionary of Twentieth Century Russian and Soviet Painters 1900 – 1980s*, Izo (1998): 313.

The Fine Arts of the Azerbaijan SSR, Sovyetsky Khudozhnik, Moscow (1978): 82 -83.

Comprehensive Art Encyclopaedia, Ed. V. M. Polyevoy, Sovetskaya Entsiklopediya Publishing House, 1986.

Painter Tagi Aziz Aga ogly Tagiev (1917 - 1993) was an honoured artist of the Azerbaijan SSR (1982). In 1935 he graduated from the Azerbaijan Art College. Between 1940 and 1941 he studied at the Moscow Art Institute.

Tagiev began exhibiting in 1933. His personal exhibitions include: Baku, 1962, 1968; Erevan, 1962; and Moscow, 1968. Tagiev's works "Lenin in the Kremlin" (1940), "Odyssey of Ker-oglu" (triptych, 1943), "Self-portrait with a carpet" (1944), and portraits of the artists B. Kengerli (1947) and S. Bakhlul-Zade (1955) are all in the collection of the Azerbaijan Museum of Art named after R. Mustafaev in Baku. Tagiev died in 1993. On the 29th of March 2013 the Baku Art Museum held an exhibition of Tagiev's work dedicated to the artist's 95th anniversary.

Meat Stew with Tomatoes and Dried Plums – *Bozartma*

Ingredients

◊ 1 kg lamb, calf or beef (brisket meat, ribs or a cut of the joint)

◊ 2 onions

◊ 6 tomatoes or 2 tablespoons of tomato paste

◊ 100 g dried plums or fresh yellow plums

◊ A handful of chestnuts

◊ 3 potatoes – chopped

◊ 1 teaspoon of turmeric

◊ Salt and pepper, to taste

Method

◊ Chop the meat into small pieces and sauté together with finely shredded onions for 10-15 minutes. Then add 3 glasses of water. Season with salt and pepper.

◊ Steam until the meat is cooked, then add the tomatoes or tomato paste, stir, add the potatoes and plums and stew until they are cooked. Instead of potatoes you can add chestnuts.

◊ Then sprinkle with turmeric and stir once again.

◊ Serve with pickles, coriander and feta cheese.

Venison with Quince Fruit
– *Maral Haiva Govurmasy*

Ingredients

◊ 1 kg venison (or wild boar)

◊ 4 onions

◊ 2 quince fruit

◊ 100 g olive oil

◊ 1 teaspoon curcuma

◊ Salt/pepper to taste

Method

◊ Cut fillet of venison into small pieces (3 x 3 cm).

◊ Cut 2 onions into small square pieces, sauté together with the venison, and add olive oil until it's half ready.

◊ Cut each quince fruit into 10-12 pieces and layer it on top of the meat.

◊ Sauté the remaining 2 onions in oil until they turn brown and layer them over the cut quince fruit. Add the curcuma on top.

◊ Add some water and stew it all together for another 40 minutes on a low heat until the meat is completely ready.

◊ Serve it with fresh green salad or marinades.

Roasted Meat
– *Govurma*

Ingredients

◊ 1 kg lamb or veal (brisket meat, a cut from the joint, quarter, shoulder)

◊ 100 g dried sour yellow plums or dried cherry plum

◊ 2 tablespoons oil

◊ 50 g unripe grape juice or lemon juice

◊ Salt and pepper, to taste

Method

◊ Cut the meat into pieces of 3 x 4 cm, not removing the bones, and sauté in the oil until browned, or if it is a fatty joint, sauté in its own juice for 10-15 minutes.

◊ Finely chop the onions, add it to the meat together with dried cherry plums or sour yellow plums. Stir continually to prevent the dish from burning. Add salt, pepper, and unripe grape juice or lemon juice.

◊ Serve with boiled or fried potatoes or with roasted tomatoes and apples, or buckwheat, or as a garnish for pilaff.

Roasted Lamb and Chestnuts
– *Et-Shabalyd Govurmasy*

Ingredients

◊ 1 kg lamb (a cut from the joint, shoulder, quarter)

◊ 2 onions

◊ 500 g of chestnuts

Method

◊ Chop the meat into small pieces, sauté in the oil (if the meat is not fat) or in its own juice until browned.

◊ Add the finely chopped onions and cook the meat, stirring occasionally. Add salt and pepper.

◊ Boil the chestnuts, then peel and mix them with the meat. Serve with fresh vegetable salad as a main course or as a garnish to pilaff.

Stuffed Cabbage Rolls with Meat in a Sweet Sauce – *Shirin Kelem Dolmasy*

Ingredients

◊ 500 g lamb or beef

◊ 1 cabbage head

◊ 2-3 onions

◊ 1 quince

◊ ½ glass rice

◊ 1 bunch each, parsley, fresh and dry mint

◊ 2 tablespoons tomato paste

◊ 1 glass of syrup from made from any jam or prepared with sugar (½ glass of sugar per 1 glass of water)

◊ ½ glass apple or grapes vinegar

◊ 1 teaspoon turmeric

◊ Salt and pepper, to taste

Method

◊ Prepare a stuffing with the meat and onions, add the washed rice, finely chopped greens, tomato paste, salt, pepper and turmeric, and stir thoroughly.

◊ Parboil the cabbage, (this way the leaves separate well), cut the leaves into thick ribs, and the larger leaves into 2 or 3 pieces.

◊ Stuff each leaf with the mixtures, make a roll and closely place in a saucepan in layers (line the bottom either with meat bones, or with thick leaves).

◊ Slice the quince and place on top.

◊ Dissolve the vinegar with syrup and pour on the dolma and cover with a lid.

◊ Boil until the rice is cooked (40-60 minutes).

◊ Optionally, you can add boiled and peeled chestnuts on top, together with the quince.

◊ Please see the following page for a variation on this classic dish.

Variation:
V Stuffed Cabbage Rolls with Walnuts – *Kor Kelem Dolmasy*

Ingredients

◊ 1 glass peeled walnuts

◊ 1 glass peeled boiled chestnuts

◊ 2 tomatoes – diced

◊ 3 onions

◊ 6 dried stoned plums

◊ 3 tablespoon vegetable oil

◊ 1 tablespoon lemon juice

◊ 1 quince

◊ 3 teaspoons rice

◊ 1 bunch basil

◊ ½ bunch coriander

◊ 1 medium cabbage head

◊ ⅓ teaspoon turmeric

◊ Salt and pepper, to taste

Method

◊ Mince the walnuts, ½ glass of chestnuts and onions; add the rice, finely chopped greens, oil, lemon juice, salt, pepper, and turmeric. Stir the mixture thoroughly.

◊ Put the cabbage in boiling water and parboil, so that the leaves can be separated easily. Stuff each cabbage leaf with 1 tablespoon of the mixture. Place in a saucepan in layers; add dried plums, slices of quince, the diced tomatoes and the rest of chestnuts on the top. Add 1½ cups of water, pour in some oil and stew until the water reduces (there should be some sauce left on the bottom).

◊ Serve with pickles, herbs, and sheep's milk cheese.

Large Meatball with Chicken, Eggs and Plums – *Ordubad Kiuftiasi*

Ingredients

◊ 1kg of lamb or veal (fillet)

◊ 200 g of turkey of chicken brisket

◊ 3 large onions

◊ ¼ glass basmati rice

◊ 10 dried or fresh cherry plums (al bukharas) or sour yellow plums

◊ 2 chicken eggs or 6 quail eggs

◊ ½ cup chickpeas

◊ 2 tablespoons of sumac

◊ 1 bunch dill

◊ Salt, pepper to taste

Method

◊ Hard boil the eggs, cool, and peel. If you're using chicken eggs, cut them into halves but leave the quail eggs whole. Soak the chickpeas for 8-10 hours in boiling water, and then boil in slightly salted water. Prepare a mixture of meat and onions (recommended to mince twice), add the washed rice, salt and pepper to taste, and stir well.

◊ Spread a piece of sterile muslin (30 x 30 cm). Form one big meatball of all the mixtures and put it in the muslin. Make a hole within the meatball for the turkey or chicken brisket meat. Insert dried cherry plum and eggs into different places of the meatball. Form the meatball once again (recommended to prepare a prolonged one) and wrap in the muslin.

◊ Put everything in a large saucepan, not destroying the shape, add the boiled chickpeas with water, and add water to cover ¾ of the meatball. Cover with the lid and boil for an hour at low temperature. Add salt, to taste.

◊ The water has to reduce and remain at the level of a half of the meatball (if the water reduces during boiling, keep it topped up).

◊ Serve in the following way: Put the meatball in a muslin in a separate dish, unwrap, and sprinkle finely chopped dill. Pour the broth with peas into a soup tureen. Serve sumac separately. Slice the meatball (as a sausage) and put in a plate with broth.

◊ Serve with pickles and fresh salads, fresh herbs – tarragon, spring onions and coriander. This dish is meant for a big family or for the holiday table. It is beautiful, unique, tasty and rich. Sometimes it is also called "Meatball a la Erzurum".

Lamb or Beef Rissoles
– *Guzu (Mal) Kotleti*

Ingredients

◊ 1 kg lamb, beef or veal

◊ 50 g brown or white bread (no crust)

◊ 2 large onions

◊ 3 cloves garlic- optional

◊ 2 tablespoons melted butter or vegetable oil

◊ 1 bunch dill

◊ Salt, to taste

Method

◊ Mince the lamb or beef, bread and onions together. Add salt and stir thoroughly.

◊ Form rissoles (7-10 pieces).

◊ Put the rissoles in a cold butter or oil in a frying pan, warm a little and move rissoles from side to side, so that they do not stick. Sauté in the oil at high temperature on both sides, so that they are juicy.

◊ Serve sprinkled with finely chopped dill. For garnish bake whole tomatoes or apples in the oven.

Roasted Meat with Onions, Quince Fruit (or Apples) and Potatoes
– *Guzu, Kartof, Haiva Govurmasy*

Ingredients

◊ 1 kg lamb veal or beef

◊ 3 onions

◊ 500 g chestnuts

◊ 10-15 dried sour yellow plums or cherry plums

◊ 4 tablespoons oil (recommended olive oil)

◊ 50 g lemon juice or unripe grape juice

◊ 4 sliced quince fruits (or apples)

◊ 4 potatoes

◊ Salt and pepper, to taste

Method

◊ Cut the meat with bones or a cut from the joint, sear in oil until browned, add the finely chopped onion and cook the meat, stirring occasionally.

◊ Cut two onions into rings and sauté in oil.

◊ Relay meat with the fried onions, dried yellow plums and sprinkle lemon juice.

◊ Stew together for 30 minutes. Add salt and pepper.

◊ Roast or fry potatoes and quince (or pan fried apples) and put everything on one serving dish.

Main Dishes - Poultry

Sattar Bakhul ogly Bakhlul-Zade

Painting: '*Baku*' (1963)

Oil on card

Signed bottom right (in Cyrillic): 'hermetil Magsuda/ khatira Satta an...';

'Sattar Bakhlul zade/1963 Baku Amiradjani village'

9.6 x 13.9 in (24.3 x 35.4 cm)

Provenance: Acquired by the current owner from the artist's family in 2001.

Literature: Bown, M. C., *A Dictionary of Twentieth Century Russian and Soviet Painters 1900 – 1980s*, Izo (1998):22.

The Fine Arts of the Azerbaijan SSR, Sovyetsky Khudozhnik, Moscow (1978): 22 – 25.

Sattar Bakhlul ogly Bakhlul-Zade (1909-1974) was born in Amiradjan, a village near Baku. He was named the People's Artist of Azerbaijan SSR, and granted the National Azerbaijan SSR award. His artistic education began in 1933 in the Drawing Department at the Moscow Surikov Fine Arts Institute, where he studied under Vladimir Favorsky. During summer workshops in the Crimea, the Russian painter Marc Chagall saw some of Bakhlul-Zade's sketches and suggested that he transfer to the Institute's Painting Department.

Bakhlul-Zade began exhibiting in 1940. His solo exhibitions include: Baku (1955, 1960, 1974), Yerevan (1956), Tbilisi (1956), Moscow (1965, 1973), and the National Gallery in Prague (1964/6). After the exhibition in Prague five of his works were selected for the museum's collection.

Chicken Stew with Onions and Quince – *Toyug Taskyababy*

Ingredients

◊ 1 whole chicken

◊ 2 onion heads

◊ 2 quince fruits

◊ ½ teaspoon citric acid or juice of 1 lemon

◊ Salt – optional

Method

◊ Cut the chicken into pieces, lay them on a pan, mix with the chopped onions, pour over 1 cup of water and add salt.

◊ Cut the quinces into slices and put them into the same pan. Stew until the chicken is ready, some broth shall remain at the bottom.

◊ Sprinkle the chicken with citric acid or spray with lemon juice. Stew for 10-15 more minutes.

◊ Serve and sprinkle with its own juice.

Main Dishes - Fish

Namik Mamed Ali ogly Zeinalov

Painting: *'Boat'* (not dated)

Oil on canvas

Signed bottom right: 'Namik'

30.4 x 34.4 in (38.6 x 38.6 cm)

Provenance: Acquired by the current owner in 1991.

Literature: Bown, M. C., *A Dictionary of Twentieth Century Russian and Soviet Painters 1900 – 1980s*, Izo (1998): 363.

Namik Mamed Ali ogly Zeinalov (1948-2009) was active in Baku, Azerbaijan.

In 2009 the Baku Arts Centre hosted an exhibition devoted to the memory of the Honoured and outstanding artist and sculptor. The works were also exposed in France, Belgium, Holland, Spain, Czech Republic, Portugal, Germany, Poland, Norway, Sweden and Austria.

Zeinalov is also the creator of a sculpture in Bruxelles "Dede Korkut" – the most famous among the epic stories of the nomadic Turks.

Sturgeon, Tuna or Swordfish Kebab – *Nere Bastyrma Kyababy*

Ingredients

◊ 2 kg fish

◊ 3 onion heads

◊ 2 tablespoons tomato paste

◊ Salt, pepper – optional

Method

◊ Cut the sturgeon into steaks, chop the onions, and mix them together. Add salt, pepper, place tightly into a pan and put it in a cool place overnight, if the weather is hot then you may wish to put it on a lower shelf of the fridge.

◊ Prior to cooking, take the pan out of the fridge and let it sit in room temperature, string the steaks on skewers, smear them with the paste, shake off the onions and cook on the brazier. Do not dry them, as this will prevent the fish from being aromatic and tender.

◊ If the fish is young basturma this is not necessary. You may cut it, add pepper and cook right away. But it will produce a completely different taste.

◊ Serve with fresh herbs, vegetables, narsharab/pome sauce, pomegranate seeds and vegetable kebabs.

Beluga with Vegetable Garnish – *Nere Buglamasy*

Ingredients

◊ 1 kg beluga or tuna for five people – you can also use tuna fish or sword fish

◊ 6 tomatoes

◊ 2 red sweet peppers

◊ 1 large courgette or aubergine

◊ 1 onion

◊ 2 carrots

◊ 1 pomegranate

◊ Salt and pepper, to taste

Method

◊ Chop all the vegetables into cubes, toss them together and cook in a little olive oil in a deep frying pan or a clay pot, do not add the water. When cooked, set aside for 25 minutes.

◊ In a hot pan, put 10 pieces of cut beluga (2 cm thick). Fry 5 minutes on each side in a little oil and top with vegetables. Cook together for 5 more minutes.

◊ Top each piece of beluga with the vegetables on a plate and decorate with pomegranate seeds.

Sturgeon/Hausen/Salmon, Pomegranate, Fresh Onions and Sumac – *Nere Bastyrmasy*

Ingredients

◊ 2 kg sturgeon, salmon or hausen

◊ 3 onions

◊ 2 pomegranates

◊ Sumac

◊ 4 tablespoons vegetable oil

◊ 4 tablespoons flour

◊ Salt – optional

Method

◊ Cut the fish into steaks (2 cm thick), add salt, roll in flour and fry on both sides in a heated pan under a lid.

◊ Cut the onion into thin rings, peel the pomegranate.

◊ Put in layers of hot fried fish, onions and pomegranate seeds. Put aside covered with a lid for several hours.

◊ Serve the fish on a plate with onion rings and pomegranate seeds on top. Sprinkle with sumac.

Steamed Sturgeon Fillet (or other white fish) – *Nere Balygy Tavada*

Ingredients

◊ 1-2 kg sturgeon, salmon or hausen

◊ 1 tablespoon turmeric

◊ Salt, to taste

Method

◊ Wash and dry the fish, generously smear with turmeric and add salt. Lay in a dip pan, pour water to cover half of the fish and cook on high heat for 20-30 minutes, then wait for the water to completely reduces on a low heat under a lid.

◊ Serve while hot with lemons, tomatoes, any boiled vegetables, pomegranate salad or pomegranate sauce.

Stuffed Caspian Fish (Kutum)*
– *Kutum Liaviangisi*

The Caspian Fish can be changed to seabass, zander, asp or pikeperch

Ingredients

◊ 1 whole black sea roach

◊ 200 g shelled nuts

◊ 2 onion heads

◊ 2 tablespoons pomegranate sauce (narsharab) or cherry-plum or plum sauce

◊ 2 tablespoons plum sauce

◊ 2 tablespoons vegetable oil

◊ 80 g sultanas

◊ 50 g dried apricots or cherry-plums

◊ 3-4 teaspoons of curcuma

◊ Salt – optional

Method

◊ Wash and dry the black sea roach.

◊ Ground the nuts, chop the onions and sauté, mix sultana, onions with nuts, dried cherry-plums or apricots and narsharab.

◊ Stuff the fish with the mixture, sew it up, smear with cherry-plum sauce or curcuma with vegetable oil. Put a tray into a preheated oven.

◊ Bake at 180°C until the top is crispy (approx. 40 minutes. Do not let the fish dry.

◊ Garnish with pomegranate seeds or sliced lemon.

Trout Fried in Oil
– Gyzarylmysh Alabalyg

Ingredients

◊ 1 trout per serving

◊ 3 tablespoons flour

◊ 4 tablespoons vegetable oil

◊ Narsharab (pomegranate sauce) or lemon

◊ Salt – optional

Method

◊ Wash and dry the trout, score the skin, add salt and flour fish on both sides.

◊ Quickly sauté on both sides in a pan with heated oil under a lid.

◊ Serve the fish hot with pomegranate sauce (narsharab) or lemon.

Main Dishes - Pilaffs

Nazim Beykishiev

Painting: *'Hut by the Sea'* (undated)

Oil on canvas

Signed bottom right: 'N. Bej'; inscription in pencil on reverse (in Cyrillic): 'N. Bekkiskiev'

30.4 x 34.4 in (77.2 x 87.3 cm)

Provenance: Acquired by the current owner in 1981.

Nazim Beykishiyev (b. 1948) is one of Azerbaijan's leading theatre artists and painters. He graduated from the A. Azimzade Art School in Baku and continued his education at the State Institute of Theatre Arts (Moscow).

Beykishiev was a member of the Union of Artists of the USSR from 1975 and, from 1979, a member of the Union of Theatre Workers of Azerbaijan. In 1984 he was awarded the State Prize of Azerbaijan for his work on Huseyn Javid's play "Iblis" (director: People's Artist of the USSR Mehti Mammadov).

In the course of his career Beykishiyev has worked in the leading theatres of Azerbaijan.

Filtered Pilaff with Soya Beans – *Mashlobiyaly Ash*

Ingredients

◊ 2 cups rice

◊ 200-300 g black sea roach or bream (sun-dried or smoked)

◊ 1 cup small brown beans (soy beans)

◊ ½ teaspoon turmeric

◊ 3 tablespoons clarified butter or olive oil

◊ 1 pomegranate

◊ Salt – optional

Method

◊ Clean the smoked black sea roach and boil it, leave it in big pieces after removing the bones. Soak the soy beans overnight, boil them and filter through a strainer. Rinse the previously soaked rice, boil for 5-7 minutes until half-cooked, strain and carefully mix with the soy beans using a skimmer.

◊ Put 1 tablespoon of oil into a pot, place the kazmag, pour a layer of rice with soy beans (1 cm thick), put the black sea roach in and cover it with remaining rice in slope shape.

◊ Sprinkle with turmeric, tightly close the pot with a lid wrapped in a cotton tissue and put the rice on a low heat to cook with this absorbtion method for 30-40 min (until the rice is ready). Then pour warm oil over it and cook for 10-15 more minutes. Serve the rice in the centre of a dish, and surround it with the fish and kazmag. This pilaff may also be accompanied with sultana and dried apricots fried in oil, fried onions, and sprinkled with pomegranate seeds.

Dough Dishes

Zakir Huseynov

Painting: '*Windy Day*' (2006)

Oil on canvas

Signed bottom left: 'Zakir'; inscription on the reverse: 'Zakir 2006/ 60 x 100'

24.8 x 39.4 in (63.0 x 100.0 cm)

Provenance: Acquired by the current owner in 2007 from the painter.

Literature: Zakir Huseynov (1951-2010), *Fərdi Sərgi, 9 dekabr 2011 - 9 yanvar 2012*, exhibition catalogue, "Хатај miniatur" gallery, 2012.

Zakir Huseynov (1951-2010) was born in Azjerbaijan. He was educated at the State College of Fine Arts named after A. Azimzade in Baku and has since had his work exhibited in Azjerbaijan, France, Russia, USA, Turkey, Australia and Georgia. Private collections of his work can be found in Azerbaijan, Russia, Germany, USA, Great Britain, Turkey, Italy, France, Canada, the Netherlands and Australia.

V Very Thin Dough stuffed with Pumpkin – *Balgabag Kutaby*

Ingredients

◊ 1 kg flour

◊ 1 egg

◊ 2 cups water

◊ Salt – optional

Stuffing:

◊ 500 g pumpkin

◊ 1 onion

◊ Seeds of 1 pomegranate

◊ 100 g butter

◊ Salt – optional

Method

◊ Prepare a stiff dough with flour, water, egg and salt, and cover with a towel. Divide the dough into balls of 5 cm, roll it into flapjacks with a diameter of 15 cm.

◊ Boil the pumpkin, then prepare a purée. Sauté the onion rings and mix with the pumpkin. Add salt.

◊ Put the stuffing on one side of the thin dough disk and cover it with the other half, pinch the edges.

◊ Sauté in oil or bake on the turned over pan for 5 minutes. When cooked, smear with the butter whilst hot.

◊ Serve with sumac and decorate with pomegranate seeds.

Ravioli with Fried Mince Meat – *Giurza*

Ingredients

◊ 500 g lamb, beef or veal

◊ 3 onion heads

◊ 100 g tail fat (as desired)

◊ 1 bunch dill

◊ Garlic-yoghurt sauce – optional

For the dough:

◊ 500 g flour

◊ 1 egg

◊ 2-2 ½ cups water

◊ Pinch of salt

◊ Salt – optional

Method

◊ Prepare the stuffing with the meat, onions and tail fat. Add salt, pepper and sauté all together.

◊ Prepare a stiff dough, roll into thickness of 3 mm, and cut circles with a glass.

◊ Put the mince meat on each circle and make a seam from both sides on the top to form a shape of snake. Leave a small opening on one end of the seam. Boil the "gurza" in broth or salty water (5-10 minutes, until the products swim up) and put on a dish with a skimmer.

◊ Pour the garlic-yoghurt sauce or some natural yogurt and sprinkle with dill. You may add 1-2 tablespoons of broth into the dish. "Gurza" can also be roasted.

Desserts and Jams

Shakhpalank Abbas ogly Mamedov

Painting: '*Autumn*' (1989)

Oil on canvas

Inscription on the reverse (in Cryllic): 'Mamedov Shakhpalank Abass og 1959 D.o.B./'Autumn' oil on canvas size 60 x 80 cm/ 1986/ 800 rubles.'

23.0 x 30.1 in (58.5 x 76.5 cm)

Provenance: Acquired by the current owner from the artist in 1989.

Literature: Bown, M. C., *A Dictionary of Twentieth Century Russian and Soviet Painters 1900 – 1980s*, Izo (1998): 199.

Painter Shakhpalank Abbas oglu Mamedov was born in 1959 and is active in Baku, Azerbaijan.

V Walnut Jam
– *Goz Miuryabbyasi*

Ingredients

◊ 1½ kg green unripe walnuts

◊ 1½ kg granulated sugar

◊ 10 carnations

◊ 2 tablespoons baking soda

◊ 1 litre water

Method

◊ Clean the green fruits from the yet soft shells and cover in water with baking soda. Wait for 2 days.

◊ Rinse thoroughly with running water, stab each nut with a fork and soak in clean water for 1 day. Rinse once more with running water, blanche for 15-20 minutes in boiling water, and strain

◊ Prepare a syrup, pour it on the nuts and boil for 30 minutes, removing the foam. Put in jars, and add a carnation. The jam will be ready after 10 days.

V Porridge from Whole Rice with Rose Water – *Yayma*

Ingredients

◊ 1 cup rice

◊ 1 litre milk

◊ 4-5 sticks saffron or 1 teaspoon cinnamon or turmeric

◊ 1 tablespoon sugar

◊ Salt – optional

Method

◊ Mix the saffron with 2 tablespoons of hot water and let it infuse under a lid.

◊ Wash the rice and cook it in milk until softened, add sugar and salt to taste.

◊ Serve on dessert plates and pour the saffron infusion over each serving or sprinkle with a pinch of cinnamon or turmeric.

◊ Serve as dessert or as a hot breakfast.

Winter

Starters – Salads and Hot and Cold Appetisers

Beyuk-Aga Meshadi ogly Mirza-Zade

Painting: '*Sketch of Ballerinas*' (undated)

Oil on canvas

Not signed; inscription on the reverse: '45 x 45 cm'

16.5 x 17.7 in (42.0 x 45.0 cm)

Provenance: Acquired by the current owner in 2011.

Literature: Bown, M. C., *A Dictionary of Twentieth Century Russian and Soviet Painters 1900 – 1980s*, Izo (1998): 209.

The Fine Arts of the Azerbaijan SSR, Sovyetsky Khudozhnik, Moscow (1978): 53-55.

Realist painter and theatre designer Beyuk-Aga Meshadi ogly Mirza-Zade (1921-2007) was born in Fatmai, near Baku, Azerbaijan. He studied at Baku Art College until 1939, and at the Moscow Art Institute before World War II. He taught at Baku Art College from the early 1940s. Having taken on an active teaching role Mirza-Zade, along with other prominent artists, took an active part in the formation of the Azerbaijani school of painting on the par with other recognized contemporary educational institutions.

Mirza-Zade is the honoured artist of the Azerbaijan SSR and the laureate of the State prize of the Azerbaijan SSR. His important shows include: 'All-Union Art Exhibition' in Moscow in 1946, 1947, 1951 and 1955.

V Cabbage Salad
– *Kelem Salaty*

Ingredients

◊ 500 g cabbage

◊ 1 cucumber

◊ 1 bunch coriander

◊ 2 tablespoons vinegar
(wine or cider)

◊ 2 tablespoons vegetable oil

◊ Salt, to taste

Method

◊ Finely shred the cabbage, salt and knead it a little bit. Dice the cucumber, chop the greens, and mix.

◊ Serve and dress with a mixture of vinegar and olive oil.

V My Mother's Cubed Aubergines
– *Ulduz Hanymyn Badymjany*

Ingredients

◊ 3 aubergines

◊ 1 onion

◊ 3 tablespoons vegetable oil

◊ Salt, pepper to taste

Method

◊ Peel and cube the aubergines, add salt and pepper, and fry in vegetable oil. Do not cover with the lid, and stir continually. Sauté until browned. Separately, finely dice the onion, and fry in vegetable oil until browned.

◊ Combine the ingredients.

◊ This recipe can be served as a hot or cold starter or as a side dish to chicken, meat or fish.

V Salad with Potato, Broccoli, Cauliflower, Cumin and Curcuma
– *Kyand Salaty*

Ingredients

◊ 1 kg baby potatoes

◊ A few florets of baby broccoli

◊ A few florets baby cauliflower

◊ 1 teaspoon cumin

◊ ½ teaspoon curcuma

◊ 1 green pepper

◊ 1 bunch of coriander

◊ 2 lemons

Method

◊ Pan fry the potatoes, steam the broccoli and cauliflower for 15 minutes and add the potatoes. Add the cumin and curcuma and leave to cook with the lid on for 10 minutes. Serve and garnish with the sliced green pepper.

◊ Add chopped coriander and squeezed lemon to taste.

V Salad with Green Beans
– *Lobiya Salaty*

Ingredients

◊   300 g fine beans (green, flat)

◊   2 tablespoons of vinegar (apple or grape) and vegetable oil each

◊   Salt and pepper, to taste

Method

◊   Cook the beans until tender, put them in a shallow dish.

◊   Dress with a mixture of fruit vinegar and olive oil, season with salt and pepper.

◊   Can be served hot or cold or as a side dish to meat or poultry.

V Omelette
– *Chalma Gayganag*

Ingredients

◊ 4 eggs

◊ 8-10 leaves spring onions

◊ 2 cloves of garlic

◊ 2 tablespoons vegetable oil or 20 g melted butter

◊ Salt and pepper, to taste

Method

◊ Finely chop the spring onions and garlic.

◊ Beat the eggs and mix them with the prepared onions and garlic, adding salt and pepper.

◊ Heat the oil in a frying pan, add the egg mixture and cover with the lid for five minutes, until the eggs are cooked through.

◊ When the eggs are cooked, serve with chopped cucumbers, tomatoes and garlic yoghurt sauce.

◊ All omelette dishes can be served as a starter or main.

Variation: Chicken Omelette
– *Toyugly Chalma Gayganag*

Ingredients

◊ 2 eggs

◊ ¼ onion

◊ ½ green pepper pod

◊ 50 g of boiled chicken

◊ 1 tablespoon vegetable oil

◊ Salt and pepper, to taste

Method

◊ Beat the eggs, add salt and pepper, and mix together with the finely chopped chicken.

◊ Heat the oil in a frying pan, add the egg mixture and cover with the lid.

◊ When the egg is cooked through, serve with chopped cucumbers and tomatoes.

V Omelette with Browned and Stewed Potatoes with Onions – *Terevez Chygyrtmasy*

Ingredients

◊ 5 potatoes

◊ 1 onion

◊ 3 tomatoes

◊ 4 eggs

◊ 1 teaspoon sumac

◊ Salt and pepper, to taste

Method

◊ Peel, wash and quarter the potatoes. Pre-fry them, then add the shredded onions and chopped fresh tomatoes, and stew for 5-10 minutes until cooked.

◊ Pour the well beaten eggs on the stewed vegetables, cover with the lid and bake for 10 minutes. Serve the cooked chygyrtma with greens, pickles and bread.

◊ Sprinkle the dish with sumac or red pepper.

V Omelette with Tomatoes
– *Pomidor Gayganagy*

Ingredients

◊ 3 eggs

◊ 3 tomatoes

◊ 1 sweet pepper

◊ 1 bunch dill

◊ 2 tablespoons vegetable oil

◊ Salt and pepper, to taste

Method

◊ Cut the tomatoes and peppers into rings and stew for 10 minutes in a frying pan. Add the oil, the beaten eggs and salt. Cover with the lid and remove from heat after 5 minutes.

◊ Sprinkle with finely chopped dill.

◊ Serve with bread, pickles and vegetables.

V French Flat Beans with Onions and Eggs – *Lobiya Gyzartmasy*

Ingredients

◊ 1 kg French flat beans

◊ 2 onions

◊ 2 eggs

◊ 4 tablespoons vegetable oil

◊ Garlic yoghurt sauce

◊ Salt, to taste

Method

◊ Finely chop the French beans, wash in a colander, boil in slightly salted water (not much, make sure the colour stays the same), and strain.

◊ Cut the onions in rings, sauté them in oil, then remove from the frying pan. Beat the eggs and cook the omelette in the oil used to fry the onions.

◊ Combine the cooked French beans and onions together in a shallow saucepan or a deep frying pan. Cover with the slices of omelette. Stew all together for about 15 minutes.

◊ Serve with garlic yoghurt sauce.

V Red Bean Salad
– *Lobiya Salaty*

Ingredients

◊ 200 g beans

◊ 2 onions

◊ 1 quince

◊ 2 tablespoons concentrated pomegranate syrup (narsharab) or balsamic vinegar glaze

◊ 2 tablespoons vegetable oil

◊ 1 bunch of coriander

◊ Salt, to taste

Method

◊ Boil the beans and strain. Cut the onions into rings and brown in vegetable oil. Finely chop the coriander.

◊ Combine all the ingredients, add the concentrated pomegranate syrup (narsharab) and sprinkle with the coriander.

◊ Serve with sheep's milk cheese and greens, and garnish with sliced quince.

◊ This can be served also as a side dish to meat and fish.

V Stewed Mushrooms with Quince and Eggs – *Kebelek Chygyrtmasy*

Ingredients

◊ 1 kg mushrooms

◊ 2 eggs

◊ 2 quince

◊ 3 tablespoons vegetable or olive oil

◊ Salt, pepper to taste

Method

◊ Stew the mushrooms whole or halved for 5 minutes.

◊ Finely dice or slice the quince into segments, roast and stew in ½ cup of water with 2 tablespoons of oil for 15-20 minutes, or until the quince becomes soft.

◊ Beat the eggs, season with salt and pepper and cook an omelette in the vegetable oil. Once cooked, cut into portions.

◊ Serve the mushrooms and stewed quince and top with the omelette.

V Aubergine Stacks with Tomatoes and Green Peppers
– *Badymjan Gatlamasy*

Ingredients

◊   4 aubergines

◊   6 tomatoes

◊   3 cloves garlic – crushed

◊   1 chilli

◊   1 sweet pepper

◊   1 bunch each dill and parsley

◊   4-5 tablespoons of vegetable oil

Method

◊   Wash the aubergines, cut them into 1cm thick rings and fry in a frying pan. Quarter the tomatoes and stew in a seperate frying pan until tender, then peel the skin. Cut the pepper into rings and sauté.

◊   Put a layer of aubergine on a dish, cover it with 2 tablespoons of tomatoes, add some fried pepper and garlic, adding salt to taste. Layer the slices in the shape of a pie.

◊   Sprinkle the finely chopped herbs on the upper layer and leave for 1 hour.

◊   Serve with the help of a palette knife.

V Steamed and Browned Carrots with Onions – *Erkioku Govurmasy*

Ingredients

◊ 500 g carrots

◊ 2 onions

◊ 1 tablespoon tomato paste

◊ Salt and pepper, to taste

Method

◊ Finely chop the 1½ onions and fry them in oil until browned.

◊ Shred the carrots, cut the remaining ½ onion in cubes and combine with the tomato paste. Stew for 15 minutes, stirring occasionally. Mix with the sauteed onions.

◊ Serve as a hot starter with fresh herbs and unsalted sheep's milk cheese.

◊ Can be also served as a side dish for meat and poultry.

V Sautéed Aubergines and Tomatoes – *Badymjan Gyimasy*

Ingredients

◊ 4 large aubergines

◊ 1 onion

◊ 1 tomato or pepper

◊ 4 tablespoons vegetable oil

◊ Salt, to taste

Method

◊ Finely dice the aubergines and onions, brown them in hot oil in a covered frying pan. Stir occasionally.

◊ After 20 minutes put the cooked aubergines and onions in a dish. Serve decorated with tomatoes, red pepper and finely chopped greens.

V Stewed Aubergines
– *Shypyrtylyg*

Ingredients

◊ 6 aubergines

◊ 500 g yoghurt

◊ 2-3 cloves garlic
(for garlic yoghurt sauce)

◊ 4 tablespoons vegetable oil

◊ ½ cup of water

◊ Salt, to taste

Method

◊ Finely cut aubergines into sticks, add to a pan with the oil, water and salt.

◊ Cover tightly with a lid, pour in some oil and stew, stirring occasionally to ensure that the vegetables do not burn, and stew for 30 minutes. The dish is ready when the water evaporates.

◊ Serve with garlic yoghurt sauce.

V Bean Paste – *Lobiya Ezmesi*

Ingredients

◊ 300 g red or spotted beans

◊ 1 onion

◊ 1 lemon

◊ 3 tablespoons vegetable oil

◊ 1 bunch of coriander

◊ Concentrated pomegranate syrup (narsharab) or balsamic vinegar glaze

◊ Salt and pepper, to taste

Method

◊ Cover the beans with boiling water. When they swell, start boiling until the beans are very soft.

◊ Mince the cooked beans with the raw onions, then add the salt, pepper, finely cut coriander, concentrated pomegranate syrup (narsharab) or juice of 1 lemon, and stir.

◊ Add the water used to cook the beans so that the dish stays very soft.

Variation: V Almond Paste – *Badam Ezmesi*

Ingredients

◊ 300 g red or spotted beans

◊ 1 onion

◊ 1 bunch coriander

◊ ½ cup crushed almonds or walnuts

◊ 4 tablespoons oil

◊ 1 tablespoon plum/cherry plum sauce or 2 tablespoons of concentrated pomegranate syrup (narsharab) or balsamic vinegar glaze

◊ Salt and pepper, to taste

Method

◊ Boil the beans, cool and mince them together with the onions and almonds.

◊ Finely chop the coriander, add the plum or cherry plum sauce, or concentrated pomegranate syrup (narsharab), and add salt and pepper.

◊ Stir well, add the oil, and sprinkle with the coriander.

◊ Add the water used to cook the beans, to ensure that the dish does not solidify.

Boiled and Chilled Sturgeon – *Nere Soyutmasy*

Ingredients

◊ 1 kg sturgeon (great sturgeon or starred sturgeon)

◊ 2 teaspoons vinegar (wine or cider)

◊ 3-4 bay leaves

◊ 10 grains bayberry

◊ 2 teaspoons turmeric

◊ Salt, to taste

Method

◊ Add cold salted water to the cooked fish, ensuring that the water completely covers the fish.

◊ Add pepper, the bay leaf, 1 teaspoon of turmeric, vinegar and boil at a high temperature for approximately 20 minutes.

◊ Take the cooked fish out of the broth, cool it down and sprinkle with the rest of turmeric.

◊ Cut the rest of the chilled fish into steaks. Serve with boiled potatoes sprinkled with finely chopped dill, sliced onions and sumac.

Lightly Salted Salmon Snack
– *Duz Ichinde Gyzylbalyg*

Ingredients

◊ 1 kg salmon fillet

◊ 200 g sea salt

Method

◊ Wash and dry the fillet, put it on a piece of cotton cloth, thickly sprinkle sea salt and envelope.

◊ Leave for a day at room temperature. Then shake the salt off, envelope in foil and put in the fridge for 2 hours.

◊ Slice the prepared fish. Serve with boiled potatoes, sour sauce with plum cherry and aubergines pickled in vinegar.

Small Puff Pastry Pies with Icing Sugar and Sumac – *Chudu*

Ingredients

◊ 500 g puff pastry

◊ 500 g lamb

◊ 2 onions

◊ 500 g olive oil or other vegetable oil

◊ 100 g sumac and icing sugar

◊ Salt and pepper

Method

◊ Prepare the mince by running the meat through a meat grinder and fry. Cut the onion into rings and sauté. Combine the meat and onions, adding salt and pepper to taste.

◊ Roll the puff pastry dough, cut into circles with a glass or plate, put 1 tablespoon of mince on each circle and make a pastry parcel with the seam on the top.

◊ Leave under a towel for 10-15 minutes.

◊ Heat all of the oil into a medium sized pot, and sauté the pastries in it by dipping them in 3-4 pieces at a time.

◊ Once cooked, remove the pastries from the oil and strain them in a colander or on a paper towel in order to remove the excess oil.

◊ When all chudu have been removed from the colander and placed on a plate, sprinkle them with the sumac and icing sugar mixture.

Soups

Soup with Artichokes, Fish and Seafood – *Balyg Artishok Shorbasy* (*Baky Shorbasy*)

Ingredients

◊ 4 onions

◊ 1 bunch parsley (or ½ cup of dried parsley)

◊ 4 cloves garlic

◊ 3 lemons – quartered

◊ 1 kg salmon or beluga

◊ 1 kg mussels

◊ 4-5 artichoke hearts

Method

◊ Finely cut the onion into rings, sauté but do not fry (onion should remain white). Sauté the garlic together with the onion, then put aside. Boil 1½ litres of water in a large saucepan, and add the fresh and already washed mussels.

◊ Once the mussels open, add the onions and garlic. Peel and half the artichokes hearts, add to the pan and add some lemons. Bring to the boil until the lemons become tender (approximately 15 minutes).

◊ Cut the fish into large pieces and add to the pan with the finely chopped parsley. Bring to the boil again for a further 5 minutes. Keep adding small amounts of water if there is not enough broth.

◊ Remove from the heat and allow the soup draw for 10-15 minutes. Serve hot.

V Soup with Beans and Thin Noodles – *Tutmaash*

Ingredients

◊ 1 cup soya/mung beans (small pinkish brown soybeans)

◊ 3 handfuls homemade thin noodles (arishta)

◊ 1 onion

◊ 2 tablespoons vegetable oil or melted butter

◊ 2 bunches coriander

◊ Salt and pepper, to taste

Method

◊ Soak the soybeans in 2 litres of water and boil until tender. Finely chop and fry the onion, and add to the broth.

◊ Add three handfuls of noodles and a little salt. When the noodles are ready, add the finely chopped coriander or dried mint.

◊ Serve with garlic yoghurt sauce (2-3 cloves of garlic mashed in 500 g of yoghurt) or fruit vinegar with or without garlic. See the page with Sauces.

Thin Noodles with Meatballs
– *Kiuftiali Arishta*

Ingredients

◊   500 g veal or lamb

◊   1 onion

◊   3 handfuls noodles
(or 2 handfuls of very thin vermicelli)

◊   1 bunch each coriander and dill

◊   Wine or cider vinegar

◊   Organic natural yoghurt (gatig)

◊   Salt and pepper, to taste

Method

◊   Wash and mince the meat together with the onion. Make small balls out of the minced meat, drop them into 2 litres of boiling water, and cook for 15-20 minutes.

◊   Add the noodles, cook until ready, adding salt and pepper to taste.

◊   Finely chop the greens and add them to the pan before serving.

◊   This soup is usually served with garlic yoghurt sauce or vinegar with garlic.

◊   Please see the following pages for variations on this classic dish.

Variation 1:
Chicken Broth with Thin Noodles
– *Toyug Arishtasy*

Ingredients

◊ 500 g chicken

◊ 1 onion

◊ 3 handfuls thin noodles
(or 2 handfuls of very thin vermicelli)

◊ 1 bunch coriander or 1
tablespoon of dried mint

◊ Salt and pepper, to taste

Method

◊ Boil the chicken in 2 litres of water. Once cooked, remove from the broth, cool, and cut into pieces.

◊ Add the thin noodles (or vermicelli) to the boiling broth. After 5 minutes add the chopped chicken, and cook for a further 10 minutes.

◊ Serve with finely chopped dill and garlic yoghurt sauce, or vinegar and garlic sauce. Garnish with the chopped coriander.

Variation 2:
V Vegetable Broth with Thin Noodles and Sauteed Onions – *Terevez Arishtasy*

Ingredients

◊ 3 handfuls noodles
(or 2 handfuls of very thin vermicelli)

◊ 2 onions

◊ 2 tablespoons vegetable oil
or butter

◊ 1 carrot

◊ 1 bunch coriander

◊ 2 tablespoons dried mint

◊ Organic natural yoghurt

◊ Salt and pepper, to taste

Method

◊ Cut the onions into thin rings and sauté them.

◊ Wash, peel, and cut carrot into circles.

◊ Boil the carrots in 1½ litres of water. Add noodles. After boiling it a little, add the sautéed onions.

◊ Sprinkle the finished dish with chopped coriander or dried mint, and add salt.

◊ Add some vinegar and garlic sauce or natural garlic yogurt sauce into each plate.

◊ Serve with fresh vegetables.

Meat Soup with Homemade Small Square-Shaped Pasta – *Sulu Hangyal*

Ingredients

◊   500 g mincemeat or diced meat (lamb, beef, or veal)

◊   2 onions

◊   3 handfuls dough cut into squares (1 x 1 cm) (recipe is provided at the beginning of the chapter)

◊   1 bunch each coriander and dill

◊   Organic natural yoghurt

◊   Salt and pepper, to taste

Method

◊   Mince the meat, chop the onions and sauté them in a pan together until it the meat browns.

◊   Pour 2 litres of water over meat and onions and cook until the meat is ready.

◊   Once the meat is cooked, add three full handfuls of dough squares into the soup. When the dough squares rise up – it means that the soup is ready. Remove the pan from the heat and immediately add the finely chopped herbs and salt.

◊   Add either: 1-2 tablespoons of garlic yogurt sauce, natural yogurt sauce, vinegar or vinegar and garlic sauce.

V Homemade Small Square-Shaped Pasta in Vegetable Broth – *Gashyg Hangyal*

Ingredients

◊ 2 onions

◊ 2 tablespoons melted butter or vegetable oil

◊ 1 carrot

◊ Dough (recipe is provided at the beginning of the chapter)

◊ 1 bunch each coriander and dill

◊ Organic natural yoghurt

◊ 2 cloves of garlic

Method

◊ Sauté the finely chopped onions and carrot in butter or oil.

◊ Add the onion and carrot mixture, and 3 handfuls of dough square to 1½ litres of boiling water, and season with salt. When the squares rise up – the soup is ready.

◊ Before serving sprinkle the soup with finely chopped herbs.

◊ Serve together with yoghurt and garlic yoghurt sauce (1-2 tablespoons into each serve).

Chicken Soup from Gyandzja with Egg Yolks and Lemon – *Gyandzja Shorbasy*

Ingredients

◊   1 whole chicken or 500 g or meat (beef, veal, or mutton, lamb)

◊   1 egg yolk

◊   1 flat tablespoon of flour

◊   1 bunch coriander

◊   2 potatoes

◊   1 onion

◊   1 medium carrot

◊   2 pinches citric acid or the juice of 1 lemon

◊   2 tablespoons vegetable oil

◊   1½ litre water

◊   Salt and pepper, to taste

Method

◊   Cook the chicken or your chosen meat until tender.

◊   Finely chop and fry the onion, cut the carrots into thin circles, halve the potatoes, and add all the vegetables to the broth. Cook until potatoes are tender.

◊   Beat the egg yolks with the flour and ½ cup of water until smooth and add it io the boiling broth, stirring it in a steady pace.

◊   Add the juice of 1 lemon or 2 pinches of citric acid.

◊   Season the finished soup with finely chopped coriander.

Meatballs from Baku
– *Baky Kiuftiasi*

Ingredients

◊ 500 g lamb

◊ 3 tablespoons rice

◊ ½ cup chickpeas

◊ 2 onions

◊ 10-15 dried cherry plums or yellow sour plums

◊ 2 eggs

◊ 2 potatoes

◊ 2 tomatoes

◊ ½ teaspoon turmeric

◊ 100 g sumac

◊ 2 teaspoons dried mint

◊ Salt and pepper, to taste

Method

◊ Mince the meat together with the onions, mix with uncooked rice, season with salt and pepper, and add the turmeric.

◊ If you have the meat bones, you can make a broth by boiling them with the pre-cooked peas, halved potatoes and fresh tomatoes.

◊ If you have no meat bones or you want to cook a light dish – you can add all the ingredients to 1½ litres of water.

◊ Make 4 balls out of minced meat. Inside each ball put half of hard-boiled egg and two cherry plums or sour plums (add the rest of the dried fruit to the broth).

◊ Cook for 20-30 minutes until the potatoes are tender. Remove the soup from heat and add dried mint.

◊ Serve with fresh greens and pickles.

◊ Serve sumac separately.

◊ Alternatively, this dish can be also cooked with veal, beef, or turkey.

Hot Yoghurt and Meatball Soup
from Gyandzja – *Kuftiali Gyandzja Dovgasy*

Ingredients

◊ 500 g meat (mutton, beef, or lamb)

◊ 1 onion

◊ 3 litres homemade natural yoghurt (gatig)

◊ ½ cup chickpeas

◊ 1 egg yolk

◊ 1 tablespoon flour

◊ 1 bunch each coriander, celery, parsley, and dill

Method

◊ Mince the meat together with the onion, mix thoroughly, and season with salt and pepper.

◊ Boil the chickpeas in advance.

◊ Wash and finely chop the herbs in advance.

◊ Mix the egg with the flour and 2 tablespoons of water until smooth. Add the cheakpeas and stir. Add the yoghurt, boiled chickpeas, and mix thoroughly.

◊ Place the mix over the heat and stir it at a steady pace until boiling.

◊ Make small balls from the meat, drop them in the boiling mixture, and cook over low heat for 10 minutes. Then add the prepared greens, and cook for another 5 minutes.

◊ Remove from heat and let it rest for 5 minutes.

◊ The dish is served hot with onions or spring onions and bread.

V Green Lentil Soup
– *Myardji Shorbasy*

Ingredients

◊   200 g green lentils

◊   2 onions

◊   2 tablespoons olive oil
or melted butter

◊   1 bunch each parsley, celery,
coriander

◊   10-15 dried cherry plums
or yellow sour plums (it's better
to use fresh fruit in summer)

◊   3 tomatoes or ½ tablespoon
of tomato paste

◊   Salt, to taste

Method

◊   Finely chop the onions and fry them in a little oil with
the chopped tomatoes or tomato paste.

◊   Boil the lentils in 5 cups of water, and add the onions
and tomatoes, chopped fresh greens, and cherry plums,
plums, or small slices of quince.

◊   When the lentils are cooked, boil everything together
for another 10-15 minutes, until soup gets thick.

◊   Once the soup has thickened, let it rest for 30 minutes.

◊   Serve with bread, herbs, and fresh vegetables.

V Potted Stew with Truffles in a Ramekin – *Dombalan Bozatmasy*

Ingredients

◊ Mushrooms – 2 truffles or 200g of other varieties of mushrooms

◊ 1 potato

◊ 1 onion

◊ 4 yellow dried plums or prunes or fresh

◊ 1 tablespoon flour

◊ 200 g sour cream

◊ Salt and pepper, to taste

Method

◊ Wash and chop mushrooms, quarter the potatoes, cut onion into rings and place in a clay ramekin with the whole plums. Add 1 glass of water.

◊ Whip the sour cream with the flour, pour the mixture into the ramekin and cover the contents with a lid. Bake in the oven for 40 minutes at a temperature of 200°C.

◊ Serve with vegetables and marinades.

Offal Dishes

Soltan Gara

Painting: *'Two Poplars and the Moon'* (undated)

Oil on canvas

Artist's symbol painted on reverse

16.1 x 13.2 in (41.0 x 33.5 cm)

Provenance: Acquired by the current owner in 1981.

Soltan Gara (1962-2011)graduated from the A. Azimzade Art School in Baku. Since 1986 he has participated in various exhibitions both in Azerbaijan and abroad. From 1988 he was a member of the Baku Centre of the Arts.

In 2000 Gara moved to the USA where he worked primarily as an interior designer. His monumental works, created in Baku in his later years, are brimming with optimism and internal harmony.

Jellied Hooves
– *Soyudulmush Hash*

Ingredients

◊ 3 sheep, cow or veal hooves

◊ 1 onion head

◊ Salt, pepper – optional

Method

◊ Clean the hooves thoroughly, cover with water, add a whole onion, aromatic pepper and stew for 5-6 hours.

◊ Remove the large bones (smaller ones may remain in the dish) and add some strong broth. Add salt to taste and allow to cool. Decorate with carrots and lemon.

◊ Serve with vinegar-garlic and garlic-gatig sauces, and sprinkle with sumac.

Steamed Hooves and Stomach – *Hash*

Ingredients

◊ 2 sheep or cow hooves

◊ 500 g stomach

◊ Vinegar-garlic sauce – optional

◊ Salt – to taste

Method

◊ Clean the hooves thoroughly, wash them, cut into joints. Clean the stomach thoroughly, cut it up into small pieces, place together into a pan and cover them with water.

◊ Stew on a very low heat for 7-8 hours without salt.

◊ Drain the broth into an enamelled pot, add salt ato taste and put the stomach and pieces of meat separated from bones into the pot.

◊ Serve hot, add vinegar-garlic sauce if desired (vinegar with mashed garlic).

Sautéed Offal with Potatoes
– *Dzhyzbyz*

Ingredients

◊ 2 kg lamb offal (lungs, liver, heart, intestine, kidneys)

◊ 300 g lamb tail fat (guyrug) or melted butter

◊ 6 potatoes – cut into fries

Method

◊ Chop 150 g of the tail fat, and prepare crackling. Wash the offal thoroughly, cut it up and put in separate pots. First, sauté the lungs in the tail fat crackling, then the liver, kidneys, and heart. Add a little salt and mix together.

◊ Then, chop the second half of the tail fat and lightly sauté. Add potatoes and fry them, then place all ingredients together in a large pot or a frying pan, mix them and hold on heat for 5 more minutes (do not burn!).

◊ Serve all the ingredients together hot, with bread, marinades, cherry salad or salads with vinegar.

Sheep's Head, Stomach and Hooves Soup – *Kelle-Pacha*

Ingredients

◊ 1 head

◊ 3-4 hooves

◊ 1 stomach

◊ Salt – optional

◊ Vinegar-garlic sauce

Method

◊ Clean the lamb head and hooves throughly, wash until white. Clean the stomach thoroughly, cover with water (the water should cover the ingredients by the thickness of 4 fingers), and cook for 7-8 hours.

◊ Then take out the large bones and serve hot with the vinegar-garlic sauce. This is a very hearty and healthy dish, which is especially good for the bones.

◊ Real gourmets consume this dish early in the morning and stay full for the rest of the day.

Main Dishes - Meat

Emin Mamedov

Painting: 'Drawing lesson 2' (2005)
Oil on canvas
Inscription on the reverse:
'19.10.2005' and a sketch of an apple
23.8 x 19.8 in (60.4 x 50.4 cm)
Provenance: Presented by artist the current owner in 2005.

Emin Mamedov was born in 1968. Emin studied at the Surikov Institute in Moscow. Now, Emin works and lives in Baku.

Minced Meat under Mashed Potato Purée – *Giymya Kartof Altynda*

Ingredients

◊ 500 g minced lamb or beef

◊ 1 large onion

◊ 4 large tomatoes

◊ 4 large potatoes

◊ 4 tablespoons vegetable oil

◊ 300 g milk

◊ Salt and pepper to taste

Method

◊ Stew the minced meat, finely chopped onions, tomatoes, salt, pepper and 1 tablespoon of vegetable oil for 25 minutes.

◊ Separately boil the potatoes. Once cooked, mash the potatoes with the milk and 2 tablespoons of vegetable oil. Mash until very soft.

◊ Place the meat and vegetables in a deep square pan, smooth and top with mashed potatoes.

◊ Place in a pre-heated oven and cook for 25 minutes at 250°C. Serve hot as a main dish.

Rabbit Stew
– *Dovshan Buglamasy*

Ingredients

◊ 1 rabbit

◊ 4 onions

◊ Salt and pepper to taste

◊ Bay leaf

◊ 4 sweet peppers

◊ 1 chilli pepper - optional

◊ 4 tomatoes

Method

◊ Cut the rabbit into pieces; put them in a deep frying pan and add bay leaf. Slice onions into thin rings and add to the pan, then stew for 20 minutes.

◊ Halve the sweet pepper place on top between the pieces of rabbit. Add the whole chilli pepper, and the halved tomatoes face down to cover the entire surface.

◊ Cover with a lid. Stew for 20 minutes until cooked and the tomatoes are soft.

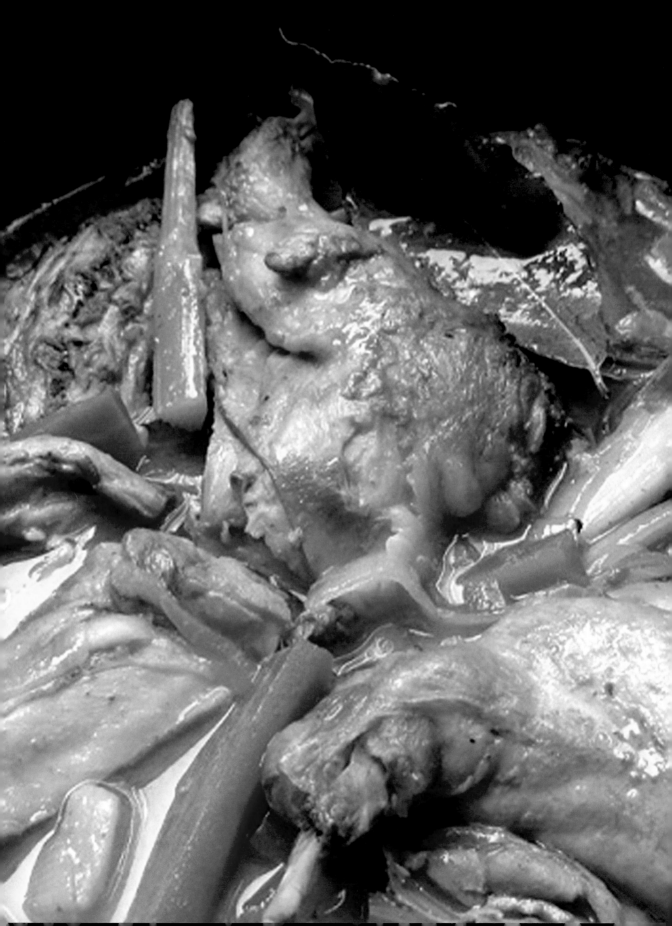

Pea Soup with Meat, Vegetables and Dry Fruit from Gyandzja – *Gyandzja Pitisi*

Ingredients

◊ 1 kg lamb, mutton or veal (brisket or shoulder)

◊ 4 potatoes

◊ 1 peeled onion

◊ ½ cup chickpeas

◊ 2 tomatoes

◊ 8-10 dried yellow prunes (optional)

◊ 3 pinches turmeric

◊ 1 large bunch dill

◊ Salt and pepper, to taste

◊ 1 white French baguette

Method

◊ Cut the meat into large pieces, and add to a pan with the peeled whole onion, pre-soaked chickpeas and dried yellow prunes. Add 2 litres of water and salt to taste.

◊ Cook firstly on a high heat, removing the scum as the mixture cooks, and then cook over a very low heat under a tight lid until the chickpeas become tender (2-3 hours). Add the halved potatoes and tomatoes and cook until the potatoes are ready, then add the turmeric.

◊ This soup can also cooked in portions in clay ramekins (pots). To do this, divide all the ingredients into 4 pieces, put the ramekins in the oven, cover tightly with a lid and cook for 3-4 hours at a temperature of 180°C. Serve in portions in a ramekin or in a bowl. Sprinkle with finely chopped dill. This pea soup can be served as two different dishes.

◊ The follow the first serving option – put everything that from the pan into bowls (meat, potatoes, peas, etc.), and cover with the broth.

◊ To follow the second option "Ishkene". When the soup is ready, remove the meat, peas, potatoes, etc. and pour the broth into bowls. Crumble churek (traditional Azerbaijani bread) or regular white French baguette in large pieces into it, and sprinkle fresh chopped dill on top. Chopped dill can be served separately.

◊ Mash everything that was in the soup with a wooden spoon, mix, sprinkle with finely chopped dill and serve as a second course with pickles and fresh greens. This dish can be cooked in the Sheki manner, replacing potato with peeled, boiled chestnuts.

Small Meat Ravioli
– *Diushbara*

Ingredients

◊ 500 g lamb, beef or veal

◊ 2 onions

◊ Dough – according to the recipe provided at the beginning of the chapter

◊ 1 tablespoon dried mint

◊ Vinegar and garlic sauce

◊ Salt and pepper, to taste

Method

◊ Mince the meat together with the onions and season with salt to taste. Roll out the dough into thin sheets and cut into squares 2 or 2.5 cm in width. Put a little meat in each square and stick corner to corner, then fasten the two ends of the resulting triangle to each other (they will look like shells).

◊ Boil 1½ litres of water, add salt, and drop ravioli into the boiling water. When the ravioli rises – the soup is ready. Before serving, add the dried mint.

◊ Serve with vinegar and garlic sauce.

◊ The same dish can be cooked in the pre-cooked chicken or meat broth. One spoon should cover around 5-8 ravioli (diushbara). If you wish, grate fresh tomatoes into the broth (1-2 tomatoes).

Pea Soup/Pottage with Meat Cooked in a Clay Ramekin – *Parcha Bozbash*

Ingredients

◊ 1 kg lamb, mutton or veal (brisket or shoulder)

◊ 2 onions

◊ ½ cup chickpeas

◊ 4 potatoes

◊ 4-5 tomatoes

◊ ½ teaspoon turmeric

◊ 2 teaspoons dill, dried mint or thyme

◊ Salt and pepper, to taste

◊ Thin lavash, pitta bread or dark rye bread

Method

◊ Cook the chickpeas in advance. Cut the meat into large pieces, finely chop the onions, and fry everything together in a pan until golden brown.

◊ Add 4 cups of water, the tomatoes, pepper, salt, and cook over a low heat until meat is tender, then add the potatoes. Add turmeric, thyme and dill to the finished thick soup.

◊ Serve with fresh vegetables or pickles, and bread (thin lavash, pitta bread or dark rye bread).

◊ This dish can be cooked in portions in the oven in clay ramekins. To do this, after sautéing the meat, put all the ingredients into 4-5 ramekins, and place them in the oven for 4 hours.

Rice Soup/Pottage with Meat and Herbs – *Shilya*

Ingredients

◊ 500 g mutton or chicken

◊ 2 medium onions

◊ ¾ cup of rice

◊ 1 bunch each of parsley, coriander, leaves of leek, spring onions, tarragon

◊ 50 g dried or 150 g of fresh cornus fruit, or 150 g of dried or fresh cherry plums or yellow sour plums

Method

◊ Cut the mutton into small pieces and fry together with the onions in a saucepan.

◊ When the meat and onions have browned, add 2 litres of water, and boil until meat is tender.

◊ Then add the purely washed rice and cornus fruit and cook until the rice is tender.

◊ Add the finely chopped greens, immediately remove the pan from heat, and cover with a lid for 5-10 minutes.

◊ The same dish can be cooked with a veal, beef, or chicken brisket.

◊ **V** As a vegetarian option this dish can be prepared without the meat, using a vegetable broth.

Azerbaijani Borsch
– *Borsch*

Ingredients

◊   1 kg brisket (veal, beef or mutton)

◊   2 carrots

◊   2 sweet peppers

◊   2 onions

◊   500 g cabbage

◊   4 tomatoes or 2 tablespoons of tomato paste

◊   2 potatoes

◊   5-6 bay leaves

◊   1 egg

◊   1 tablespoon flour

◊   2 lumps sugar

◊   1 bunch parsley and celery each

◊   2 tablespoons each of vinegar and vegetable oil or melted butter

◊   Salt and pepper, to taste

Method

◊   Sauté the finely chopped onions, carrots, peppers, tomatoes (seasonally) or tomato paste to brown in vegetable oil.

◊   Cook the brisket until tender in 2 litres of water, remove the froth from the broth, and remove the meat.

◊   Add the potatoes, chopped cabbage, and sautéed dressing to the broth.

◊   Beat the egg yolk with the water and flour until smooth and pour it into the borsch, stirring it in a steady pace.

◊   Add the vinegar (wine or cider) and sugar.

◊   Turn off the heat, add the finely chopped herbs, meat, and cover the pan with a lid.

◊   Serve with sour cream.

Meatballs from Gyandzja
– *Gyandzja Kiuftiasi*

Ingredients

◊ 500 g mutton (meat only)

◊ 2 tablespoons rice

◊ 5-10 leek or spring onions leaves

◊ 1 bunch each of basil, mint, parsley, dill, coriander

◊ 2 onions

◊ ½ cup chickpeas

◊ 10-15 dried sour yellow plums or dried cherry plums

◊ 2 tomatoes (optional)

◊ 2 eggs

◊ 2 potatoes

◊ 1½ teaspoon turmeric

◊ Salt and pepper, to taste

Method

◊ Mince the meat together with onions.

◊ Thoroughly mix the raw rice and finely chopped fresh greens with the minced meat, season with pepper. Cook the chickpeas and eggs separately, and peel the eggs once cooked.

◊ Cook the meat broth using the meat bones and add pre-cooked chickpeas to it.

◊ Make 4 meatballs and press a plum or a cherry plum together with half a hard boiled egg into each one.

◊ Add the meatballs and halved potatoes to the boiling broth and – if you wish – add the finely chopped fresh tomatoes.

◊ Boil until potatoes and rice are ready. Then remove the pan from heat, add the turmeric and some chopped fresh dill. Serve pickles, fresh herbs and sumac separately.

◊ To make a lighter dish, cook the meatballs and potatoes not in the broth, but in 2 litres of water.

◊ To make the dish with beef or veal, the recipe is the same.

Meatballs with Quince
– *Sulu Kiufta*

Ingredients

◊ 700 g lamb, veal or beef

◊ 2 tablespoons tomato paste

◊ 1 quince (or 1 potato, depending on the season)

◊ 3 onions

◊ Salt and pepper, to taste

Method

◊ Mince the meat and 2 of the onions, make small meatballs, and put them in a saucepan with boiling water (1 litre).

◊ Finely chop and fry the remaining onion, slice the quince and potatoes and combine all the ingredients together in a saucepan with the tomatoes or tomato paste. Add salt and pepper, to taste.

◊ Stew for 30 minutes, stirring occasionally.

Mini Meatballs in Pomegranate Juice with Onions and Walnuts – *Fisindjan*

Ingredients

◊ 500 g lamb, veal or beef (a cut of the joint)

◊ 1 cup meat broth

◊ 2 onions

◊ 1 cup peeled walnuts

◊ 50 g fresh cherry plum or pomegranate juice

◊ 2 tablespoons oil

◊ 1 pomegranate

◊ Salt, to taste

Method

◊ Mince the meat and onion, add salt, and make mini meatballs approximately the size of a cherry and sauté in the oil.

◊ Mince the walnuts and sprinkle them on the meatballs.

◊ Add cherry plums, cherry extract, sour pomegranate juice, or lemon juice, and 1 cup of broth and stew together for 10 minutes.

◊ Garnish the dish with pomegranate seeds and serve with with mixed salad or as a side dish to pilaff.

Meatball Omelette
– *Tava Kyabab*

Ingredients

◊ 500 g boneless lamb, beef or veal

◊ 2 onions

◊ 4 eggs

◊ 2 tablespoons oil

◊ Salt and pepper, to taste

Method

◊ Prepare a mixture of meat and onions, season with salt and stir thoroughly.

◊ Form meatballs the size of a walnut from the mixture and flatten them to form small flat round rissoles and lightly sauté them on both sides. Once cooked, add them to a frying pan with the beaten in eggs, adding salt and pepper to taste.

◊ Cover with the lid, and when the eggs have set, the dish is ready to serve.

◊ Serve with fresh green salad and herbs (in winter – with pickles).

Mince Meat with Onions
– *Giymya*

Ingredients

◊ 1 kg boneless lamb, beef or calf

◊ 4 onions

◊ 2 tablespoons vegetable oil or melted butter

◊ ½ teaspoons turmeric

◊ Salt, to taste

Method

◊ Mince the meat and two onions, season with salt and pepper and stew under a lid for 10 minutes.

◊ Cut the rest of the onions into rings and fry in the oil or butter. Add the prepared meat mixture and sauté together until cooked.

◊ This can be served with many dishes – noodles, pilaff, Hangyal or as a separate dish with French fries or fried tomatoes.

◊ See recipes for Filtered Pilaff (Siuzmya Ash) on page 96 for a suitable side dish and Sulu Hangyal on page 356.

Chilled Lamb
– *Soyutma*

Ingredients

◊ 2 kg lamb (shoulder bones, round bones, from the hind quarters, cannon bones with meat)

◊ 1 onion

◊ Sumac

◊ 1 bunch each of dill and parsley,

◊ Salt and pepper, to taste

Method

◊ Cut the lamb into pieces at the joints and put them in a saucepan full of water together with a whole peeled onion. The water should cover the meat. Boil under the lid at low temperature for 1 hour until the meat is cooked.

◊ When the meat is cooked, serve it whilst it's still hot. Add enough pepper and a sprinkling sumac.

◊ Garnish with boiled vegetables or potatoes.

◊ Serve with fresh herbs and sour cherry or tomato salad. (Please see section on salads).

Small Meatcakes Stewed with Tomatoes, Onions and Potato
– *Gazan Kotleti*

Ingredients

◊ 500 g lamb fillet

◊ 4 onions

◊ 5 potatoes

◊ 2-3 tablespoons tomato paste or 3 tomatoes

◊ Salt and pepper, to taste

Method

◊ Mince the meat together with one of the onions. Stir thoroughly. Cut the rest of the onions into rings and put in the bottom of a saucepan.

◊ Make meatcakes from the meat mixture approximately 3 cm in diameter. Place them on the layer of onions, and cover them with the layer of chopped potatoes. Add salt. If possible, place everything in several layers (onions, meat pancakes and potatoes).

◊ Cover the last layer with grated tomatoes or tomato paste, add ½ cup of water and stew for an hour at a low temperature.

Mutton or Lamb Stew
– *Taskyabab*

Ingredients

◊ 1 kg lamb, veal, or beef

◊ 4 onions

◊ ½ teaspoon turmeric or 1 tablespoon thyme

◊ 1 pomegranate

◊ Salt and pepper, to taste

Method

◊ Cut the meat into large pieces. Cut the onions into rings and add to the meat, and add a little salt.

◊ Add 1 cup of water, and if the water reduces add a little more, and stew at a low temperature until the meat is cooked. Do not stir.

◊ Season the cooked meat with turmeric or thyme.

◊ Serve with the sauce from the meat broth and onions from the bottom of the pan.

◊ Peel and de-seed the pomegranate and garnish the dish with the seeds.

◊ It is possible to serve this dish as a garnish for any type of pilaff.

Sautéed Meat and Aubergines – *Et Musambasy*

Ingredients

◊ 1 kg lamb, veal or beef (front quarter, brisket meat)

◊ 3 onions

◊ 4 aubergines

◊ 3 pinches citric acid or the juice of 1 lemon

◊ 1 teaspoon turmeric

◊ 2 tablespoons vegetable oil

◊ Salt and pepper, to taste

Method

◊ Cut the lamb and one onion into small pieces, add ½ cup of water and sauté. Don't cook it through until the end.

◊ Cut the remaining onions into rings, add salt and fry together.

◊ Peel and slice the aubergines into 1 cm pieces, add salt and coat with oil. Sauté on both sides in a frying pan, covered with the lid, at a high temperature until par-cooked.

◊ Put the lamb on one side of a deep frying pan or copper saucepan, and the aubergines on the other side. Cover with a layer of the fried onions, sprinkle with the citric acid or lemon juice and stew under the lid at low temperature for 30 minutes, until the meat is cooked.

◊ Add the turmeric 10 minutes before the meat is cooked.

◊ Serve with vegetables, fresh salads, herbs or as a garnish to pilaff. (Please see recipe for Filtered Pilaff on page 96).

Main Dishes - Poultry

Tahir Salahov

Painting: 'Still Life with Jars' (1977)

Oil on canvas

55x64cm

Provenance: acquired from a private collection in 2012

Tahir Salahov was born in Baku in 1928. After studying at the Azimzade Art College (1945–1950) and the Surikov Moscow Art Institute (1951-1957), he gained early recognition as his diploma work was exhibited at the Moscow All-Union Art Exhibition in 1957, receiving public and critical acclaim.

He became one of the leading exponents of the so-called "severe style", a trend in 1960s Soviet art that aimed to set off a hard, realist view against the ceremonial "polished reality" of that era.

Today Salahov is a practising artist and professor at the Moscow Art Institute. He has received numerous honours, including People's Artist of USSR, Hero of Socialist Labour, Vice-President of the Russian Academy of Arts, member of over 20 academies and other creative organizations throughout the world.

Sautéed Chicken with Aubergines and Onions – *Toyug Musambasy*

Ingredients

◊ 1 kg chicken

◊ 2 onions

◊ 4 aubergines

◊ 3 pinches citric acid or the juice of 1 lemon

◊ 1 teaspoon turmeric

◊ 2 tablespoons vegetable oil

◊ Salt and pepper, to taste

Method

◊ Cut the chicken into pieces, add ½ cup of water and stew until it is half cooked.

◊ Cut the onions into rings, add salt and sauté together.

◊ Peel and slice aubergines 1 cm pieces, add salt to each of them and coat with oil. Sauté on both sides in a frying pan covered with a lid, at a high temperature until par-cooked.

◊ Put the chicken on one side of a deep frying pan or copper saucepan, and the aubergines on the other side. Cover with the layer of fried onions, sprinkle with the citric acid or lemon juice and stew under the lid at low temperature for 30 minutes, until the meat is cooked.

◊ Add the turmeric 10 minutes before the chicken is cooked.

◊ Serve with vegetables, fresh salads, herbs or as a garnish for pilaff. (Please see recipe for Filtered Pilaff on page 96).

Stuffed Chicken, Duck or Pheasant with Nuts and Dry Fruit – *Liaviangi*

Ingredients

◊ 1 whole chicken or duck or pheasant

◊ ½ cup walnuts

◊ 1 onion

◊ 5-6 dried cherry-plums

◊ 1 tablespoon narsharab or balsamic vinegar glaze (not balsamic vinegar)

◊ 1 tablespoon olive oil

Method

◊ Salt the chicken on the inside and outside. Run the nuts and raw onion through a meat grinder, mix with the narsharab (or balsamic vinegar glaze or cherry-plum extract). Stuff the chicken and sew it up. Smear with cherry-plum extract and oil.

◊ Wrap the bird in aluminium foil and place on a tray

◊ Bake at 180°C for 1 hour, adding 4 cups of water to the tray to keep the bird from drying out.

◊ Serve hot or cold

◊ Salt – optional

Liaviangi: Variation of Stuffing

Ingredients

◊ 1 whole chicken or duck or pheasant

◊ 1 cup walnuts or almonds

◊ 1 onion,

◊ 50g raisins (or sultanas) and 50g dried apricot

◊ 2 tablespoons oil

◊ 1 pomegranate

Method

◊ Fry the onions, mix with ground walnuts or almonds and add water to create a soft mixture, adding pomegranate seeds, raisins or sultanas and chopped apricots. Stuff the bird and sew it up.

◊ Wrap the bird in aluminium foil

◊ Place the stuffed bird on a tray with ½ cup of water and bake at 180°C for 40-50 minutes. The same stuffing may be used for chicken or any other bird.

◊ You can also add albukhara (dried plum) to the stuffing.

Chicken (or Turkey) with Ground Nuts and Plum Sauce or Lemon Juice – Toyug Fisindjany

Ingredients

◊ 1 kg chicken or turkey tenderloin

◊ 1 cup shelled walnuts (or almonds)

◊ ½ cup cherry-plum or plum sauce or juice of 1 lemon

◊ Oil

◊ Salt and pepper – to taste

Method

◊ Chop the chicken into small pieces (2 x 2 cm), add salt and pepper to taste.

◊ Stew in a pan on a low heat after adding ½ cup of water. When the chicken is ready, reduce the water, add the oil and grounded nuts, fry it all until browned, stirring continuously.

◊ Garnish with the cherry-plum sauce or lemon juice, and stew for 5 more minutes.

◊ Serve 5 minutes later hot, or allow to cool and serve.

Main Dishes - Pilaffs

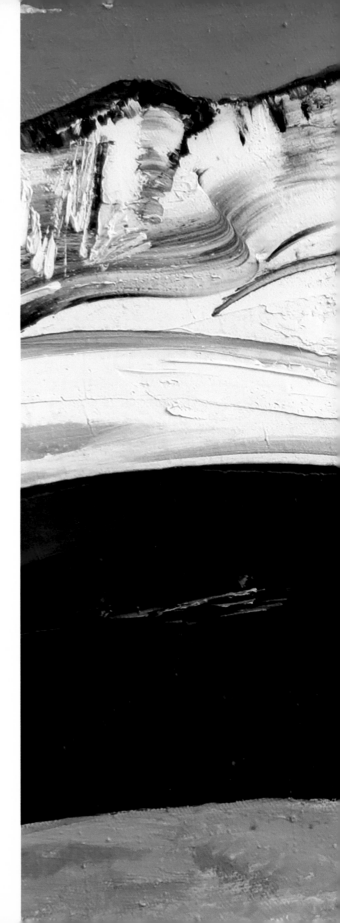

Nadir Sadykh ogly Kasumov

Painting: '*Snowy Mountains*' (1979)

Oil on canvas

Signed and dated in bottom right corner (in Cyrillic): 'N. Kasumov 79'; inscription on the reverse (in Cyrillic): 'N. Kasumov Snowy Mountains'

15.7 x 19.7 in (40.0 x 50.0 cm)

Literature: Bown, M. C., *A Dictionary of Twentieth Century Russian and Soviet Painters 1900 – 1980s*, Izo (1998): 131.

The Fine Arts of the Azerbaijan SSR, Sovyetsky Khudozhnik, Moscow (1978): 40 – 42.

Nadir Sadykh ogly Kasumov (1928-2002) was born in Baku and is an honoured artist of the Azerbaijan SSR. He studied at the Baku Azimzade Art College between 1941 and 1946. Kasumov's teachers at this time were recent graduates of the Surikov Art Institute in Moscow - talented young painters and graphic artists - Sattar Bakhlul-Zade, Mikhail Abdullayev and Beyukaga Mirza-Zade. They taught the young man to understand constructive solid form, strict and decisive sculpting using large blocks of colour, as well as the creation of forms using colour. Amongst his works of this period are: portraits of famous artists and leaders of manufacture, pictures dedicated to the miners, cotton growers, rice growers and builders. In 1953 he graduated from the Repin Institute of Art, Sculpture and Architecture in St Petersburg.

V Draught Milk Pilaff with Sweet, Dried Fruits – *Siudlu Ash*

Ingredients

◊ 2 cups jasmine or basmati rice

◊ 300 g dried fruits (persimmon, dried apricots and sultana)

◊ 1 litre milk

◊ 5-6 sticks saffron or 1 teaspoon turmeric

◊ 2 tablespoons butter/oil (butter, olive oil or vegetable oil)

◊ Salt – optional

Method

◊ Prepare a saffron infusion by mixing the saffron with 1 tablespoons of boiling water, cover and let it infuse for 10-15 min.

◊ Boil the milk and add the previously soaked and rinsed rice and saffron, cover the pan with a lid wrapped in a towel and put on low heat. The milk should evaporate.

◊ After 20 minutes put all dried fruits in the middle of rice, cover it with a lid and cook on a low heat using an absorbtion method for 30 minutes on a very low heat until the rice is ready. Add the oil or butter and cook for an additional 10-15 minutes.

◊ Serve on a dish with the dried fruits, and separately serve the sugar. The crust that forms at the bottom is also served on the dish.

Green or Brown Lentil Filtered Pilaff with Black Sea Roach – *Mardjili Ash*

Ingredients

◊ 2 cups rice

◊ 200-300 g black sea roach, salmon, mackerel or bream (sun-dried or smoked)

◊ 1 cup green or brown lentils

◊ ½ teaspoon each cumin and turmeric

◊ 3 tablespoons oil (any kind)

◊ Salt – optional

Method

◊ Clean the black sea roach cut it into small pieces and boil. Cook the lentils in salty water and filter through a strainer.

◊ Rinse the previously soaked rice, boil in salty water for 5-7 minutes until half-cooked, then filter through a strainer. Put 1 tablespoon of oil into a pot, and place the kazmag. Carefully mix the rice with the lentils and fish using a skimmer and place it in the pot. Sprinkle with turmeric and cumin.

◊ Tightly close the pot with a lid wrapped in a cotton tissue and put the rice on a low heat to cook for 30-40 minutes. Then pour hot oil over it and cook this absorbtion method for 10 more minutes. Once cooked, serve the pilaff on a large dish.

◊ This pilaff may also be accompanied with sultana and dried apricots fried in oil, fried onions, and sprinkled with pomegranate seeds.

◊ **V** A vegetarian alternative can be made by omitting the fish from the dish.

Filtered Pilaff with Stuffed Poussin or Quail – *DioshiamyaToyug Siuzmya Ash*

Ingredients

◊ 4 cups rice

◊ 1 whole poussin or 2 whole quails

◊ 2 onions

◊ 100 g sultanas/raisins

◊ 4 tablespoons butter or olive oil

◊ 0.5 g saffron

◊ ½ teaspoon cumin or zira

◊ 100g butter

◊ 1 pomegranate

◊ Salt, pepper – optional

Method

◊ Half-cook the poussin, adding salt and pepper to taste. The leftover broth may later be used for preparation of another dish.

◊ Fry the onion rings (prepare Sogancha), and mix with the sultanas and pomegranate seeds. Stuff the poussin with the mixture and wrap it in a muslin. Mix the saffron with 2 tablespoons of boiling water and let it infuse.

◊ Rinse the rice soaked overnight and boil in salty water, for 5-7 minutes until half-cooked and filter through a strainer.

◊ Prepare a kazmag, place it on the bottom of the pot onto the oil, add a layer of rice 1 cm thick and lay down the bird, cover it with the remaining rice in a slope, sprinkle with cumin or zira, add the saffron and tightly close with a lid wrapped in a cotton tissue.

◊ Cook on a low heat for 40 mins, then pour warm oil over it and cook using this absorbtion method for another 10-15 minutes.

◊ Serve the pilaff (try to place the layer of rice with saffron on the top). Chop the chicken into pieces and serve on a separate plate.

◊ Serve on a large place or in individual portions. Serve with marinades, green onions, tarragon, rayhan (basil) and green salads with vinegar.

Fresh Dill or Dried Fennel Filtered Pilaff with Large White Beans – *Chuyut-Pakhla Ash*

Ingredients

◊ 4 cups rice

◊ 1 kg lamb or veal (brisket)

◊ 2 bunches fresh dill
(or 2 teaspoons dry fennel)

◊ 4 tablespoons clarified butter

◊ 1 pomegranate

◊ 200 g large white beans

◊ Salt, pepper – optional

Method

◊ Soak the rice in salty water overnight and boil the beans in advance.

◊ Cut the meat into large pieces and boil it, adding salt and pepper to taste, then wrap in a muslin.

◊ Chop the fresh dill. Rinse the rice, boil 5-7 minutes until half-cooked, then filter through a strainer. Mix with dill (or fennel) and boiled white beans.

◊ Prepare a kazmag, put it on the bottom of a pan on oil. Add a layer of rice (1 cm thick) and cover it with the meat, then add the remaining rice in a slope. Cover with a lid wrapped in cotton cloth.

◊ Cook on low heat for 40 minutes. Then add warm oil and cook using this absorbtion method for an additional 10-15 minutes. Serve the rice and meat on a dish, and sprinkle with pomegranate seeds.

◊ Serve with bagyrbeyin or liver paté (page 66).

◊ V A vegetarian alternative can be made by omitting the lamb from the dish.

V Thin Vermicelli Filtered Pilaff – *Arishteli Ash*

Ingredients

◊ 200 g Arishta (very thin homemade vermicelli) or thin noodles

◊ 2 cups rice

◊ 0.5 g saffron

◊ ½ teaspoon cumin

◊ 1 egg

◊ 3 tablespoons vegetable oil or clarified butter

◊ Salt – optional

Method

◊ Break the vermicelli or noodles into small pieces, approximately 1 or 2 cm in size and fry it until browned Prepare a saffron infusion by mixing the saffron with 2 tablespoons of boiling water and cover it with a lid.

◊ Rinse the previously soaked rice, boil in 2 litres of water with the noodles or vermicelli for 5 minutes until half-cooked, then filter through a strainer.

◊ Put 1 tablespoon of oil in a pan, place the lavash or stiff dough, add the rice with noodles, cumin and saffron infusion, tightly cover with a lid wrapped in cotton towel and put on a low heat.

◊ After 25 minutes make a small deepening in the centre of the rice and crack the egg into it. Cover the egg with rice and continue cooking for an additional 20 minutes, then add the rest of the oil and stew for an additional 10 minutes.

◊ Serve with marinades, vegetable and green salads.

Dough Dishes

Oleg Ibrahim ogly Ibrahimov

Painting: '*Man in the doorway of a house*' (undated)

Oil on composite board

Signed in black paint bottom left (in Cyrillic): 'Ibragimaov'

15.7 x 19.7 in (40.0 x 50.0 cm)

Provenance: Presented by artist for the current owner in 1981.

Literature: Bown, M. C., *A Dictionary of Twentieth Century Russian and Soviet Painters 1900 – 1980s*, Izo (1998): 113.

Oleg Ibrahim ogly Ibrahimov was born in Baku in 1943 to the family of the poet Ibrahim Kabirli. After completing high school, the gifted young man studied at the Moscow Surikov Institute and the Mukhina Leningrad Higher School of Industrial Art.

In 1976, as part of the Central Committee of the Communist Youth League at the height of the Brezhnev era, the young artist was sent to the Baikal-Amur Mainline, whose grand-scale construction project later inspired a lot of his work. Back in Moscow, Ibrahimov opened his solo exhibition at the "Manezh" exhibition space, which caused great enthusiasm amongst the Soviet press. Ibrahimov is also a member of the USSR Guild of Artists.

In 2008 Ibrahimov had his solo show in the "Yaradan" exhibition hall in Baku. His paintings have also been exhibited in Moscow and St.Petersburg in the framework of the Decade of Azerbaijani Culture in the Russian Federation, as well as in the best salons in Finland, Morocco, Bulgaria, Poland, Germany, the Czech Republic and other countries.

Diamond-shaped Pasta with Meat
– *Giymali Siuzmya Hangyal*

Ingredients

◊   1 kg flour

◊   1 egg

◊   3 onions

◊   800 g lamb, veal or beef

◊   3 tomatoes or 1 tablespoon of tomato paste

◊   3 tablespoons oil

◊   Garlic-yoghurt sauce

◊   Salt – to taste

Method

◊   Prepare the mince meat and onions together then sauté with chopped tomatoes (giymya).

◊   Prepare a stiff dough with flour, egg, a pinch of salt and 2-2½ cups of water.

◊   Knead the dough, divide into balls the size of a tennis balls and roll each ball until the dough becomes as thin as 3 sheets of paper.

◊   Then cut the dough into diamonds 5-6 cm in size and pat them dry.

◊   Boil diamond shaped pieces and then strain.

◊   Serve with the garlic-gatig sauce and add giymya (sauté mince meat and onions). Garnish with pomegranate seeds.

Very Thin Dough Stuffed with Meat
– *Et Kutaby*

Ingredients

◊ 1 kg flour

◊ 1 egg

◊ 2 cups water

◊ 500 g meat (lamb, veal)

◊ 4 onions

◊ 1 pomegranate

◊ Salt – optional

Method

◊ Prepare a stiff dough with flour, egg, a pinch of salt and water, cover it with a towel.

◊ Prepare mince with the meat and onions. Peel the pomegranate.

◊ Cut the dough into balls with a diameter of 5 cm, roll it into thin disks with the thickness of 2 sheets of paper and the size of a dessert plate. Put a thin layer of mince meat on one side of the disk, sprinkle with pomegranate seeds (5-6 seeds) and cover the meat with the other half of the disk, pinch the edges.

◊ Sauté in oil on both sides or bake on both sides on a large, turned upside down pan on a high heat.

◊ When the kutaby are ready, smear them with butter on both sides and stack them. The same dough is prepared for all kutaby types.

V Roasted Vermicelli with Sugar or Honey – *Hopmaja*

Ingredients

◊ 500 g vermicelli

◊ Granulated sugar or honey

◊ Salt – optional

Method

◊ Sauté then boil the dry fine vermicelli in salty water and filter through a strainer.

◊ Make a slope in an aluminium pan, cover with a lid wrapped in cotton cloth, put on low heat for 20 min.

◊ Serve with separate granulated sugar (1 teaspoon or tablespoon per serving) or honey.

Desserts

Oleg Ibrahim ogly Ibrahimov

Painting: *'Candle'* (1980)

Oil on canvas

Signed in black paint bottom left (in Cyrillic): 'Ibragimaov'

15.7 x 19.7 in (40.0 x 50.0 cm)

Provenance: Purchased from the artist's studio.

Literature: Bown, M. C., *A Dictionary of Twentieth Century Russian and Soviet Painters 1900 – 1980s*, Izo (1998): 113.

Oleg Ibrahim ogly Ibrahimov was born in Baku in 1943 to the family of the poet Ibrahim Kabirli. After completing high school, the gifted young man studied at the Moscow Surikov Institute and the Mukhina Leningrad Higher School of Industrial Art.

In 1976, as part of the Central Committee of the Communist Youth League at the height of the Brezhnev era, the young artist was sent to the Baikal-Amur Mainline, whose grand-scale construction project later inspired a lot of his work. Back in Moscow, Ibrahimov opened his solo exhibition at the "Manezh" exhibition space, which caused great enthusiasm amongst the Soviet press. Ibrahimov is also a member of the USSR Guild of Artists.

In 2008 Ibrahimov had his solo show in the "Yaradan" exhibition hall in Baku. His paintings have also been exhibited in Moscow and St.Petersburg in the framework of the Decade of Azerbaijani Culture in the Russian Federation, as well as in the best salons in Finland, Morocco, Bulgaria, Poland, Germany, the Czech Republic and other countries.

V Dense Buttery Confection with Sesame Seeds – *Kiunjiut Halvasi*

Ingredients

◊ 100 g sesame seeds

◊ 300 g granulated sugar

◊ 1½ cup water

◊ 6 tablespoons olive oil

Method

◊ Fry the sesame seeds, boil a thick syrup with sugar and add it to the sesame seeds while still hot. Add some oil and fry the thinck mixture for a few minutes.

◊ Pour onto a plate at 1 cm thickness layer. Allow to cool and serve.

V Doughnuts
– *Kopmadja*

Ingredients

◊ ½ teaspoon baking soda

◊ 200g organic natural yoghurt

◊ 2 eggs

◊ Flour, depending on the toughness (so it is the consistency of sour cream)

◊ 1-2 teaspoons sugar sand

Method

◊ Mix the yoghurt and sugar in a bowl, slowly add the eggs to the mixture.

◊ Add ½ teaspoon of baking soda to a teaspoon of wine vinegar before combining with flour into the bowl. Mix well.

◊ Heat a frying pan with olive oil on a maximum heat. Add the mixture to the frying pan and reduce the heat.

◊ As the doughnuts start to rise slightly, turn them in the frying pan and fry the other side, adding plenty of olive oil to the pan.

◊ Serve while hot with sour cream, feta cheese and honey. These can be served for either breakfast or dessert.

V Small Walnut Rolled Pastry
– *Miutekke*

Ingredients

◊ 250 g sour cream

◊ 3 cups flour

◊ 1 egg yolk

◊ ⅓ teaspoon carbonate

◊ 1 teaspoon vinegar

◊ Vanilla, enough to cover the tip of a knife

◊ 1 cup shelled walnuts

◊ 1 cup granulated sugar

◊ A pinch of salt

Method

◊ Beat the sour cream with the egg yolk, add the vanilla, mix the carbonate with vinegar and pour it into the sour cream, add flour and knead the dough.

◊ Run the nuts through a meat grinder and mix with granulated sugar.

◊ Roll the dough out thinly and cut up into triangles. Put a spoon of stuffing on the base of each triangle and roll it up to the upper corner.

◊ Bake for 15-20 minutes at 180°C.

V Dense Buttery Confection with Saffron – *Rakhtarbeish*

Ingredients

◊ 500 g rice chaff

◊ 2 cups water

◊ 1 tablespoon saffron infusion

◊ 100 g shelled walnuts
or almonds

◊ 100 g granulated sugar

◊ Salt – optional

Method

◊ Boil the rice chaff in water until completely ready, add the granulated sugar and a little salt.

◊ Mix with the ground nuts, saffron, and serve on small plates while hot.

V Sweet Bread
– *Shekerchorek*

Ingredients

◊ 200 g butter or margarine

◊ 1 cup granulated sugar

◊ 2 egg yolks

◊ ⅓ teaspoons carbonate of soda

◊ 1 tablespoon vinegar

◊ One pinch of vanilla

◊ 3½ cups flour

Method

◊ Beat the butter with most of the yolks using a mixer. Add the sugar, vanilla and carbonate with vinegar and mix once again.

◊ Add the flour to the mixture and knead to a stiff dough. Make balls the size of a small egg, squash a little, and smear the centre with yolk.

◊ Bake on a tray at 180°C for 30 minutes.

◊ Carefully serve using a spatula.

V Deep Fried Filo Pastry
– Bishi

Ingredients

◊ 2 cups flour

◊ Water – as much as it takes

◊ 1 egg yolk

◊ 100 g sumac

◊ 100 g icing sugar

◊ 750 g vegetable oil

◊ Salt – optional

Method

◊ Prepare a dough with the flour, yolk and water and roll in thin layers (2 mm). Cut the layers into stripes, and make roses or bows.

◊ Dip into the boiling oil, fry to a brownish colour, and serve. Mix the sumac with the icing sugar and sprinkle over the bishi generously.

V Pahlava from Rice Flour with Nuts and Coriander Seeds – *Irishta Pahlavasy*

Ingredients

For the dough:

◊ 300 g rice flour

◊ Water

◊ Salt

For the stuffing:

◊ 700 g walnuts or hazelnut

◊ 3 g coriander seeds

Separately:

◊ 1 g saffron

◊ 400 g granulated sugar

◊ 300 ml water

Method

◊ Mix the rice flour, salt and water thoroughly (the dough should be a density of a thick sour cream). Pour the dough onto an oiled tray in the form of a net and bake the layer for 5 minutes, this layer is called irishta. 6-8 layers should be prepared.

◊ For the stuffing: run the nuts through a meat grinder, mix them with the granulated sugar and ground coriander seeds.

◊ Stack the layers, spreading all nuts stuffing between the layers.

◊ Decorate the top layer with the saffron infusion in the shape of a net (2 tablespoons of hot water for 1 g of saffron). This is best applied with a brush.

◊ Bake in the oven for 15-20 minutes.

◊ Dissolve the granulated sugar in water, boil it and soak the pahlava with the syrup.

◊ Let it rest for 8-10 hours, then cut the pahlava into diamond shapes and serve.

V Porridge from Rice Flour
– Firni

Ingredients

◊ 4 tablespoons rice flour

◊ 1 litre milk

◊ 2 tablespoons sugar

◊ 3 tablespoons rose water
(tea rose extract) or 1 teaspoon
cinnamon

◊ 2-3 sticks saffron

◊ Salt – optional

Method

◊ Mix the rice flour and milk, add sugar, salt. Boil while stirring to prevent lumps on a low heat until it thickens to the density of semolina.

◊ Add the rose water, sprinkle the cinnamon and serve on dessert plates. Add a drop of saffron essence in the centre (pour two tablespoons of boiling water on the saffron sticks and soak for 10-15 minutes).

◊ Serve while hot or cold for dessert or for breakfast.

V Sweet Refreshing Drink with Basil Seeds – *Baleng (Sherbet)*

Ingredients

◊ 2 tablespoons basil seeds

◊ 1 litre water

◊ 500 g granulated sugar

◊ 200 g rose water or 5-6 drops of rose oil

Method

◊ Boil water and sugar to make a syrup.

◊ Pour the hot syrup over the basil seeds and leave overnight.

◊ Add the rose water before serving.

◊ Serve cold with pilaffs and kebabs.

Marinades and Sauces

Without the traditional marinades and sauces it is impossible to imagine the national cuisine of Azerbaijan. Vinegar, seasonings and greens are used in the preparation of marinades and sauces.

For example, the vinegar marinade has a specific soft and unusual taste. Sauces are normally made of berries – cherry-plum, plum, cornus fruit, and stored in the form of sauce, as well as in the form of paste.

The narsharab sauce prepared with pomegranate is a perfect seasoning for meat and fish, and the vinegar-garlic and gatig-garlic sauce enhances the dishes with an extraordinary taste.

Azerbaijani dishes need very little salt, because spices and seasoning greens, dry extracts and sauces from cherry-plums and plums of various kinds, as well as cherries and cornus fruit are used everywhere. Also, during the summer season, many fresh sour fruits are used (cherry-plum, plum, cherry, cornus fruit, pomegranate, quince). All marinades and sauces need to be composed of the freshest ingredients.

Below is the list of most used dry grasses and seeds: zira, cumin, sumac, dried spearmint, thyme, dried rosemary, turmeric, dried basil, anise, cinnamon, estragon, snake fern.

V Aubergine Marinade with Herbs and Garlic – *Badymdjan Turshusu*

Ingredients

◊ 2 kg medium aubergines

◊ 2 bulbs garlic

◊ 3-4 long green peppers or chillis

◊ 5-6 large bunches parsley or celery

◊ 500 g grape or cider vinegar

◊ 2 teaspoons salt

Method

◊ Remove the stalk from the aubergines wash them, make longitudinal cuts down the centre. Add to boiling water, blanch for 10 minutes, then remove them and press with a lid in strainer for several hours.

◊ Wash and dry the greens and peppers. Chop and peel the garlic, and mash or cut into thin circles. Then mix the greens, pepper and garlic thoroughly.

◊ Add salt to the inside of each aubergine, then cut and fill with the mixture. Put the aubergines in layers tighly into jars, so that the stuffing does not fall out, and fill with the vinegar. In 3-4 days the marinade is ready. Put in a cool place for storage.

V Marinade with Squash
– Patison Shorabasy

Ingredients

◊ 1 kg (preferably small) squash

◊ 1 cup vinegar

◊ 3-4 bay leaves

◊ 6-7 pieces of allspice

◊ ½ teaspoon salt

Method

◊ Wash the squash (if they are large – quarter them), scald with boiling water and put them into a jar.

◊ Mix the vinegar with ½ cup of water and a little salt. Boil and fill the squash to the top.

◊ Put a bay leaf into the jar with a little pepper, and leave in the dark for two days. Then transfer to the fridge.

V Marinade from Different Vegetables – *Hevtebedjer Shorabasy*

Ingredients

◊ 500 g cabbage

◊ 2 carrots

◊ 1 bunch each celery, parsley

◊ 1 green chilli

◊ 2 bell peppers

◊ 500 g fruit or wine vinegar

◊ 1 teaspoon coriander seeds

◊ 1 teaspoon salt

Method

◊ Wash all the vegetables, cut them into small pieces (longitudinally, in squares or circles), and the greens into 2 cm pieces. Mix everything and add tightly to a jar and fill with vinegar to the top.

◊ The marinade is ready after 5-6 days.

◊ Any types of vegetables and greens (except for green onions) may be added to this marinade in various proportions. Depending on the selection of vegetables, greens and proportions, different tastes are achieved.

V Marinated Flat Green Beans
– *Lobiya Shorabasy*

Ingredients

◊ 2 cups fruit vinegar

◊ 300 g green flat French beans

◊ 6 green peppers

◊ 3 carrots

◊ 100 g celery stems

◊ 1 teaspoon salt

Method

◊ Remove the stems from the beans and peppers, and blanche for 10-15 minutes in a vinegar solution (1 tablespoon of vinegar to ½ cup of water).

◊ Peel the carrots and cut longitudinally into 4-5 pieces, and wash the celery stems. Put the ingredients tightly in a jar and add salt. Fill with vinegar to the top.

◊ The marinade is ready in 5-6 days. It can be prepared without the carrots.

V Red Cabbage Marinade
– *Gyrmyzy Kelem Shorabasy*

Ingredients

◊ 1 kg cabbage

◊ 4 small beetroots

◊ Salt – optional

Method

◊ Cut the cabbage into pieces (3 x 3 cm).

◊ Peel and cut the beetroots into thin round slices, add salt and mix everything.

◊ Put tightly in the jar, add ½ cup of warm water and salt. As it brews the cabbage will sink to the bottom, therefore it needs to be supplemented. Leave in a warm place.

◊ Ready in 4-5 days.

V Marinated White Cabbage, Pepper and Herbs – *Bibar-Kelem Gey Turshusu*

Ingredients

◊ 1 kg each of white cabbage and green long peppers

◊ 5 large bunches celery or parsley

◊ 500 g wine or fruit vinegar

◊ 2 teaspoons salt

Method

◊ Cut the cabbage in large pieces (5 x 5 cm), lay on a towel and let it dry for 12 hours.

◊ Wash the pepper, remove the stalk, and boil in ½ cup of water and 1 cup of vinegar. When boiling, dip the pepper and blanche for 5-10 minutes. Allow to cool.

◊ Wash and dry the greens, chop into 2.5 - 3 cm pieces.

◊ Then tightly put in layers into the jars: first the cabbage, then the pepper, celery, and so on in layers until the jar is full. Press each layer down as you go, and add salt to taste with each layer.

◊ Fill to the top with vinegar (use the vinegar remaining from blanching the pepper) and leave it for several days at room temperature.

◊ Put the jar in a bowl, because the marinade may fall out when the cabbage brews.

◊ When the cabbage sinks down, vegetables should be used to top it up.

◊ In 4-5 days the marinade is ready.

◊ Store in a cool place.

◊ Please see the following pages for variations on this classic recipe.

Variation 1:
V Marinated Red and Green Peppers
– *Bibar Turshusu*

Ingredients

◊ 1 kg green long peppers

◊ 4 red sweet pepper

◊ 700 g wine or fruit vinegar

◊ 1 bunch celery or coriander

◊ 2 teaspoons salt

Method

◊ Remove the stalk from the peppers. Cut the red pepper into rings and blanche in a vinegar solution for 10 minutes, add salt to taste. Remove and mix with the chopped celery.

◊ Put tightly into the jar and fill with vinegar used for blanching the peppers, if the jar is not full – add more vinegar.

◊ Ready in 2 days.

Variation 2:
V Marinated Cabbage and Celery
– *Kelem-Kereiuz Turshusu*

Ingredients

◊ 1 – 1½ kg white cabbage

◊ 2 large bunches celery

◊ 3 carrots

◊ 500g wine or fruit vinegar

◊ ½ teaspoon cumin

◊ 2 teaspoons salt

Method

◊ Cut the cabbage in large pieces (4-5 cm). Wash and dry the celery, and chop into 2-3 cm pieces.

◊ Peel and cut the carrots into thin round pieces.

◊ Press the cabbage, mix with the celery and carrot, sprinkle with cumin, add salt to taste and pour into the jar by pressing tightly, and fill the jar with vinegar. As it sinks down, add more cabbage and celery.

◊ When brewing the marinade may fall out, therefore put the jar in a bowl or pot.

◊ Leave at room temperature for 4-5 days, then store in a cool place.

V Marinated Garlic
– *Sarymsag Shorabasy*

Ingredients

◊ 2 kg garlic

◊ 500 g fruit vinegar

◊ 2 teaspoons coriander seeds

◊ 1 teaspoon cumin

◊ 1 small beetroot

◊ 3 teaspoons salt

Method

◊ Scald the garlic cloves with boiling water, put into jars, add coriander seeds and cumin slices, add salt and fill with vinegar to the top.

◊ Add beetroot for the colour, if pink garlic is desired. If not then cook without the beetroot.

◊ Ready to be consumed after 5-6 days.

V Marinade with Green Tomatoes, Garlic and Green Peppers – *Yashil Pomidor Shorabasy*

Ingredients

◊ 1 kg green tomatoes

◊ 1 bulb garlic

◊ 300 g green pepper or chilli

◊ 1 cup vinegar

◊ 4-5 bay leaves

◊ 1 teaspoon salt

Method

◊ Wash and scald the tomatoes and pepper. Remove the stalk from the pepper and peel the garlic.

◊ Put the tomatoes in the jars with the pepper, garlic and bay leaf among the tomatoes.

◊ Mix the vinegar with a cup of water, boil it, add salt and pour into the jars with the vegetables. If not enough – add vinegar. Ready to be consumed in 5-6 days.

V Tomato Sauce
– *Pomidor Gabarmasy*

Ingredients

◊ 2 kg tomatoes

◊ 4 onions

◊ 1 hot pepper

◊ 4 tablespoons vegetable oil

◊ Salt – optional

Method

◊ Peel the tomato skin (scald them with boiling water), chop up and put on to stew.

◊ Chop the pepper and add it to the tomatoes. Chop the onions, sauté in oil, then add to the tomatoes and stew for 20-30 minutes.

◊ This sauce may be stored long term in jars.

◊ Please see below for a variation on this classic recipe.

Variation 1:
V Sauce with Tomatoes, Onions and Parsley – *Pomidor, Sogan, Gey Gabarmasy*

Ingredients

◊ 2 kg tomatoes

◊ 1 hot pepper

◊ 1 bunch parsley

◊ 4 onions

◊ 4 tablespoons vegetable oil

◊ Salt – optional

Method

◊ Peel the tomatoes, dice them and stew. Chop the pepper and add to the tomatoes.

◊ Cut the onions in rings and fry until browned, then add to tomatoes and stew for 20 minutes.

◊ Chop the parsley into the boiling mixture and turn off the heat immediately.

V Yellow or Green Sour Plum Sauce
– *Alycha Turshusu*

Ingredients

◊ 5-6 kg cherry-plums

◊ ½ cup water

◊ 2 teaspoons salt

Method

◊ Wash the cherry-plums, put in a pot, add water and stew under a lid on a low heat. After 15-20 minutes, when the berries are soft, rub them through a strainer.

◊ Put the mixture into a non-stick pot and stew while continuously stirring, until the mixture becomes thick.

◊ 30 minutes later add salt to the sauce, put it in jars and use as needed.

◊ Sauce may be served with meat or chicken. It may be prepared from ripe cherry-plums of any kind, but it is better to use large yellow and green cherry-plums.

Variation 1:
V Sauce with Cherry-Plums and Garlic
– *Alycha-Sarymsag Turshusu*

Ingredients

◊ 5-6 kg cherry-plums

◊ 5 cloves garlic

◊ ½ cup water

◊ 2 teaspoons salt

Method

◊ Put the ripe cherry-plums in a large pot, add the water, cover with a lid and stew on a low heat for 15-20 minutes. When the berries are soft rub them through a strainer.

◊ Put the mixture into a non-stick pot and stew while continuously stirring until the mixture thickens, then add salt.

◊ When the sauce is ready add the mashed garlic and mix. This sauce is served only for dinners. If one bunch of parsley is chopped into the sauce another variant of sauce may be achieved. The same recipe may be used to prepare sauces with plum and blackthorn.

V Pomegranate Sauce
– Narsharab

Ingredients

◊ 4 kg pomegranate

Method

◊ Squeeze the juice out of unpeeled pomegranates, put it on the heat and reduce it to half its initial volume, stirring occasionally.

◊ Serve with fish and meat dishes.

◊ The sauce should be thick like jam syrup.

◊ The sauce has a sour-sweet taste.

◊ Sauce may be stored for a long time in a cool place.

◊ You can buy it ready-made in the shops – similar to a balsamic vinegar glaze (not balsamic vinegar).

V Spearmint Sauce
– *Iskendzhevi*

Ingredients

◊ 1 cup water

◊ 4 tablespoons granulated sugar

◊ ½ cup fruit or vine vinegar

◊ 1 bunch spearmint

Method

◊ Mix the water with the sugar and vinegar, dip the spearmint into this solution and boil it. Put the sauce in the fridge after cooling.

◊ Serve with crisp head lettuce as a starter (the salad is dipped into the sauce).

V Garlic Sauce with Homemade or Organic Yoghurt – *Sarymsagly Katyk*

Ingredients

◊ 500 g katyk

◊ 3-4 cloves garlic

Method

◊ Mash the garlic, and mix with katyk.

◊ Allow to rest for 30 minutes.

V Vinegar-Garlic Sauce
– *Sirke-Sarymsag*

Ingredients

◊ 4 cloves garlic

◊ 300 g wine or cider vinegar

Method

◊ Mash the garlic and mix with the vinegar.

◊ Allow to rest for 30 minutes.

V Sautéed Chopped Onions in Oil – *Sogancha*

Ingredients

◊ 4-5 onions

◊ 4 tablespoons vegetable oil or clarified butter

◊ Salt – optional

Method

◊ Peel the onions, cut them in thin rings, add salt, and put in a pan with the oil. Cover with a lid and stew for 10 minutes. Then take the lid off and allow to brown.

◊ This sauce may be used for sandwiches, as well as served with meat and poultry dishes.

V Extract from Rose Petals
– Giulab

Ingredients

◊   2-3 kg petals of tea rose or briar flowers

◊   500 g icing sugar

Method

◊   Normally prepared by method of dripping, but can also be prepared in home conditions. Mix the rose petals with the icing sugar in glass bowl and store in sunlight. Drain the juice periodically.

◊   When the juice stops coming out – strain through sterile cheesecloth, pour into bottles and seal them. Add sherbet, confectionery, namely to pahlava.

◊   Decreases high blood pressure.

V Extract from Mulberry
– *Bekmez*

Ingredients

◊ 3 kg mulberry

◊ ½ cup water

Method

◊ Place the washed mulberry in a pot, add water, and put on the heat. When the water starts to boil and the mulberry releases its juice, throw it in a strainer and rub the fruits through it.

◊ Boil the strained fruits, stir continually until it thickens to the density of watery sour cream and is dark-brown in colour.

◊ Pour into bottles.

◊ The mulberry syrup – bekmez – is very helpful against coughs or anaemia (1 tablespoon 3 times a day).

V Extract from Grapes – *Doshab*

Ingredients

◊ 5-6 kg grapes

◊ ½ cup water

Method

◊ Put the washed grapes in a pot, add water and boil completely.

◊ Boil the mass to the density of watery sour cream with dark-brown colour. Pour into bottles.

V Juice from Unripe Grapes
– Abgora

Ingredients

◊ 5 kg green grapes

Method

◊ Wash the green unripe grapes, dry thoroughly. Squeeze the juice through a cotton cloth.

◊ Pour into jars, and store in the sun.

◊ After 2 months, without stirring up the residue, pour the clear liquid in bottles and put in cool place.

◊ Serve with meat dishes to add a sour taste.

◊ This is a great treatment for blood pressure (drink 1 teaspoon 3 times a day for one month).

Tahir Salahov

Painting: 'A Mexican Corrida' (1969)

Oil on canvas

75x86cm

Provenance: acquired from a
private collection.

Tahir Salahov was born in Baku in 1928.
After studying at the Azimzade Art College
(1945–1950) and the Surikov Moscow
Art Institute (1951-1957), he gained early
recognition as his diploma work was
exhibited at the Moscow All-Union Art
Exhibition in 1957, receiving public and
critical acclaim.

He became one of the leading exponents
of the so-called "severe style", a trend in
1960s Soviet art that aimed to set off a
hard, realist view against the ceremonial
"polished reality" of that era.

Today Salahov is a practising artist and
professor at the Moscow Art Institute.
He has received numerous honours,
including People's Artist of USSR, Hero
of Socialist Labour, Vice-President of the
Russian Academy of Arts, member of
over 20 academies and other creative
organizations throughout the world.

Additional Recipes

These are the additional recipes that I have been cooking for my grandchildren in the recent months.

V Baku Olivier Salad

Olivier Salad used to be one of the most popular salads in the former Soviet Union. However each republic (there used to be 16 of them) prepared the salad depending on their climate and local customs. In Baku this salad used to be cooked the following way:

Ingredients

◊ 500 g beef of chicken breast

◊ 4 potatoes

◊ 2 medium cucumbers

◊ 1 jar of marinated cucumbers

◊ 2 carrots

◊ 4 green apples

◊ 1 onion

◊ 0.5 kg of fresh-frozen green peas

◊ 2 jars of sour cream

◊ 1 big bunch of parsley or coriander

◊ Salt and pepper, to taste

Method

◊ Boil the meat, cool it down and slice into small pieces (1 x 1 cm).

◊ Boil potatoes, peel them, cool down and cut (1 x1 cm).

◊ Boil carrots, cool them down and cut (1 x 1 cm).

◊ Peel and cut apples (1 x 1 cm)

◊ Cut fresh cucumbers (1 x 1 cm).

◊ Cut marinated cucumbers (1 x 1 cm).

◊ Peel and cut the onion (1 x 1 cm).

◊ Scald the green peas; place them in a colander and strain.

◊ Chop the parsley finely.

◊ Mix all ingredients with sour cream. Add pepper.

◊ V * For a vegetarian dish simply do not add any meat.

V Olivier Salad in a Shell

Ingredients

◊ Olivier Salad – 1 kg

◊ Buy ready brioches – 20 pieces

Method

◊ Cut the tops of brioches.

◊ Put as much Olivier Salad inside the brioches as you can.

◊ Cover each brioche with its top.

◊ Serve as an appetiser or a cold snack. Beautiful and tasty.

V Oven-baked Turkey Breast
– *Hind Gushu Sobada*

Ingredients

◊ 1 turkey breast (preferably a big piece)

◊ 100 g olives, green or black

◊ 50 g almonds

◊ 5-6 cloves of garlic

◊ 1 jar of sour cream

◊ Salt, pepper

Method

◊ Stuff the turkey breast with olives, almonds and garlic – make the holes with a sharp knife and insert almonds, garlic and olives.

◊ Add enough salt and pepper.

◊ Coat with a think layer of sour cream.

◊ Wrap in foil and put into a hot oven (200°C) for 3 hours.

◊ Pour 1 litre of water into the baking tray. If the water evaporates, add some more.

◊ In 3 hours open the foil, leave to cool down and cut into thin slices. Serve as a snack or a sandwich filler.

Lumu Sherniyati

Ingredients

◊ 6 lemons

◊ 0.5 kg of granulated sugar or 0.5 kg of honey (clear and not thick)

Method

◊ Cut the lemons into thin circles without peeling the rind.

◊ Put in a jar.

◊ Cover with granulated sugar or honey.

◊ Leave to infuse for 2-3 days.

◊ Lemons will release juice and melt the sugar.

◊ You will have a very beautiful desert.

◊ It is very good for children from 2 years old for good appetite and haemoglobin.

Bal Goz Shirnijati

Ingredients

◊ 0.5 kg of honey (clear and not thick one is better)

◊ 300 g walnuts (peeled)

Method

◊ Mix walnuts with honey, leave to infuse for 1 day and serve with a desert and a cup of tea. Very good for haemoglobin. Specially recommended to expecting mothers.

Published in 2015 by
Unicorn Press Ltd
66 Charlotte Street
London
W1T 4QE
www.unicornpress.org

Text © Khabiba Kashkay
Artwork © The named artists

English Language ISBN: 978-19065-09927
Russian Language ISBN: 978-19100-65211

10 9 8 7 6 5 4 3 2 1

Book production by Lucy Duckworth and Felicity Price-Smith
Project managed by Rena Lavery
Printed in China on behalf of Latitude Press